DOVER · THRIFT · EDITIONS

Selections from the Journals

HENRY DAVID THOREAU

Edited by WALTER HARDING
Founding Secretary, The Thoreau Society

DOVER PUBLICATIONS, INC.
New York

DOVER THRIFT EDITIONS

GENERAL EDITOR: STANLEY APPELBAUM
EDITOR OF THIS VOLUME: WALTER HARDING

Copyright

Published in Canada by General Publishing Company, Ltd., 30 Lesmill Road, Don Mills, Toronto, Ontario.

Published in the United Kingdom by Constable and Company, Ltd., 3 The Lanchesters, 162–164 Fulham Palace Road, London W6 9ER.

Bibliographical Note

Selections from the Journals is a new selection, first published by Dover Publications, Inc., in 1995. The text is taken from *The Journal of Henry D. Thoreau*, edited by Bradford Torrey and Francis H. Allen and published by the Houghton Mifflin Company in 1906. The present selection and Note were prepared specially for the Dover edition by Walter Harding.

Library of Congress Cataloging-in-Publication Data

Thoreau, Henry David, 1817–1862.
   [Journal. Selections]
   Selections from the journals / Henry David Thoreau ; edited by Walter Harding.
      p.   cm. — (Dover thrift editions)
   ISBN 0-486-28760-2 (pbk.)
   1. Thoreau, Henry David, 1817–1862 — Diaries. 2. Authors, American — 19th century — Diaries. 3. Natural history — Massachusetts — Concord. I. Harding, Walter Roy, 1917– . II. Title. III. Series.
PS3053.A2   1995
818'.303 — dc20
[B]
                                                     95-12191
                                                       CIP

Manufactured in the United States of America
Dover Publications, Inc., 31 East 2nd Street, Mineola, N.Y. 11501

Note

WHEN HENRY THOREAU (1817–1862) graduated from Harvard College and returned to his native Concord, Massachusetts, in 1837, he first met Ralph Waldo Emerson, who had recently moved to the town. Emerson, already well-established in his literary career, recognized Thoreau's potential as a writer and urged him to start keeping a daily journal as a source for material, as Emerson had for a number of years. Thoreau started his own journal that very day, October 22, 1837, and kept it up for twenty-five years until his final illness, a few months before his death. While he began the journal as a source of material, much of which was used in his books, he gradually saw the journal as a work of art in itself and began writing it as such. Whereas he had not hesitated literally to gut the earlier journal to obtain material for A Week and Walden, scissoring out long passages, he now left his journal intact. The result is a fascinating record of his thoughts as they developed over a long period of time. How he ever thought it could be thus published when he had great difficulty in getting his short essays published, we do not know. However, he had faith in himself and in his work. Although none of this journal was published in his lifetime, efforts to get it published were begun almost immediately upon his death. His friend H. G. O. Blake of Worcester, who had inherited the manuscript journal through Thoreau's sister Sophia, published four volumes of excerpts from the journal in the 1880s and 1890s. The full journal was published in 1906 and has been reprinted many times since. Although the journal is ideally read complete, many people are overwhelmed by the thought of reading fourteen volumes of more than two million words. And so I have created this one-volume sampler, hoping that it may entice its readers to go on to the full work. I have made no attempt to miniaturize

the journal as a whole, covering its various topics in the exact propor-
tions of the original, but have rather chosen some of my favorite selections.

It matters little, I believe, whether one reads this volume straight
through or by dipping in here and there. Whichever approach the
reader uses, he will become acquainted with a fascinating personality —
one unique in American literature. Thoreau writes with verve and vigor.
His prose is some of the most poetic in our language. He writes both
with great humor and fine seriousness. He writes on a wide variety of
subjects. Many people think of him primarily as a naturalist and it is true
that he is often concerned with natural history. But that is not his only
subject. He writes even more about man — man in general, man in
Concord and about one particular man — Henry David Thoreau himself. I am pleased to introduce you to the fascinating journal of one of
America's greatest writers.

WALTER HARDING

1837

(ÆT. 20)

Oct. 22. "What are you doing now?" he asked. "Do you keep a journal?" So I make my first entry to-day. . . .

Oct. 29. Two ducks, of the summer or wood species, which were merrily dabbling in their favorite basin, struck up a retreat on my approach, and seemed disposed to take French leave, paddling off with swan-like majesty. They are first-rate swimmers, beating me at a round pace, and — what was to me a new trait in the duck character — dove every minute or two and swam several feet under water, in order to escape our attention. Just before immersion they seemed to give each other a significant nod, and then, as if by a common understanding, 'twas heels up and head down in the shaking of a duck's wing. When they reappeared, it was amusing to observe with what a self-satisfied, darn-it-how-he-nicks-'em air they paddled off to repeat the experiment. . . .

1841

Jan. 30. . . . Fair Haven Pond is *scored* with the trails of foxes, and you may see where they have gambolled and gone through a hundred evolutions, which testify to a singular listlessness and leisure in nature.

Suddenly, looking down the river, I saw a fox some sixty rods off, making across to the hills on my left. As the snow lay five inches deep, he made but slow progress, but it was no impediment to me. So, yielding to the instinct of the chase, I tossed my head aloft and bounded away, snuffing the air like a fox-hound, and spurning the world and the

1

Humane Society at each bound. It seemed the woods rang with the hunter's horn, and Diana and all the satyrs joined in the chase and cheered me on. Olympian and Elean youths were waving palms on the hills. In the meanwhile I gained rapidly on the fox; but he showed a remarkable presence of mind, for, instead of keeping up the face of the hill, which was steep and unwooded in that part, he kept along the slope in the direction of the forest, though he lost ground by it. Notwithstanding his fright, he took no step which was not beautiful. The course on his part was a series of most graceful curves. It was a sort of leopard canter, I should say, as if he were nowise impeded by the snow, but were husbanding his strength all the while. When he doubled I wheeled and cut him off, bounding with fresh vigor, and Antæus-like, recovering my strength each time I touched the snow. Having got near enough for a fair view, just as he was slipping into the wood, I gracefully yielded him the palm. He ran as though there were not a bone in his back, occasionally dropping his muzzle to the snow for a rod or two, and then tossing his head aloft when satisfied of his course. When he came to a declivity he put his fore feet together and slid down it like a cat. He trod so softly that you could not have heard it from any nearness, and yet with such expression that it would not have been quite inaudible at any distance. So, hoping this experience would prove a useful lesson to him, I returned to the village by the highway of the river. . . .

Feb. 18. . . . It is the unexplored grandeur of the storm which keeps up the spirits of the traveller. When I contemplate a hard and bare life in the woods, I find my last consolation in its untrivialness. Shipwreck is less distressing because the breakers do not trifle with us. We are resigned as long as we recognize the sober and solemn mystery of nature. The dripping mariner finds consolation and sympathy in the infinite sublimity of the storm. It is a moral force as well as he. With courage he can lay down his life on the strand, for it never turned a deaf ear to him, nor has he ever exhausted its sympathy. . . .

April 5. . . . I only ask a clean seat. I will build my lodge on the southern slope of some hill, and take there the life the gods send me. Will it not be employment enough to accept gratefully all that is yielded me between sun and sun? Even the fox digs his own burrow. If my jacket and trousers, my boots and shoes, are fit to worship God in, they will do. Won't they, Deacon Spaulding? . . .

1842

March 26. . . . I must confess I have felt mean enough when asked how I was to act on society, what errand I had to mankind. Undoubtedly I did not feel mean without a reason, and yet my loitering is not without defense. I would fain communicate the wealth of my life to men, would really give them what is most precious in my gift. I would secrete pearls with the shellfish and lay up honey with the bees for them. I will sift the sunbeams for the public good. I know no riches I would keep back. I have no private good, unless it be my peculiar ability to serve the public. This is the only individual property. Each one may thus be innocently rich. I inclose and foster the pearl till it is grown. I wish to communicate those parts of my life which I would gladly live again myself. . . .

1845–47

[Undated] . . . From all points of the compass, from the earth beneath and the heavens above, have come these inspirations and been entered duly in the order of their arrival in the journal. Thereafter, when the time arrived, they were winnowed into lectures, and again, in due time, from lectures into essays. And at last they stand, like the cubes of Pythagoras, firmly on either basis; like statues on their pedestals, but the statues rarely take hold of hands. There is only such connection and series as is attainable in the galleries. And this affects their immediate practical and popular influence. . . .

1850

[Undated] . . . I once set fire to the woods. Having set out, one April day, to go to the sources of Concord River in a boat with a single companion, meaning to camp on the bank at night or seek a lodging in some neighboring country inn or farmhouse, we took fishing tackle with us that we might fitly procure our food from the stream, Indian-like. At the shoemaker's near the river, we obtained a match, which we had forgotten. Though it was thus early in the spring, the river was low, for there had not been much rain, and we succeeded in catching a mess of fish sufficient for our dinner before we had left the town, and by the shores of Fair Haven Pond we proceeded to cook them. The earth was uncommonly dry, and our fire, kindled far from the woods in a sunny recess in the hillside on the east of the pond, suddenly caught the dry grass of the previous year which grew about the stump on which it was kindled. We sprang to extinguish it at first with our hands and feet, and then we fought it with a board obtained from the boat, but in a few minutes it was beyond our reach; being on the side of a hill, it spread rapidly upward, through the long, dry, wiry grass interspersed with bushes.

"Well, where will this end?" asked my companion. I saw that it might be bounded by Well Meadow Brook on one side, but would, perchance, go to the village side of the brook. "It will go to town," I answered. While my companion took the boat back down the river, I set out through the woods to inform the owners and to raise the town. The fire had already spread a dozen rods on every side and went leaping and crackling wildly and irreclaimably toward the wood. That way went the flames with wild delight, and we felt that we had no control over the demonic creature to which we had given birth. We had kindled many fires in the woods before, burning a clear space in the grass, without ever kindling such a fire as this.

As I ran toward the town through the woods, I could see the smoke over the woods behind me marking the spot and the progress of the flames. The first farmer whom I met driving a team, after leaving the woods, inquired the cause of the smoke. I told him. "Well," said he, "it is none of my stuff," and drove along. The next I met was the owner in his field, with whom I returned at once to the woods, running all the way. I had already run two miles. When at length we got into the neighborhood of the flames, we met a carpenter who had been hewing timber, an infirm man who had been driven off by the fire, fleeing with his axe. The farmer returned to hasten more assistance. I, who was spent with running, remained. What could I do alone against a front of flame half a mile wide?

I walked slowly through the wood to Fair Haven Cliff, climbed to the highest rock, and sat down upon it to observe the progress of the flames, which were rapidly approaching me, now about a mile distant from the spot where the fire was kindled. Presently I heard the sound of the distant bell giving the alarm, and I knew that the town was on its way to the scene. Hitherto I had felt like a guilty person, — nothing but shame and regret. But now I settled the matter with myself shortly. I said to myself: "Who are these men who are said to be the owners of these woods, and how am I related to them? I have set fire to the forest, but I have done no wrong therein, and now it is as if the lightning had done it. These flames are but consuming their natural food." (It has never troubled me from that day to this more than if the lightning had done it. The trivial fishing was all that disturbed me and disturbs me still.) So shortly I settled it with myself and stood to watch the approaching flames. It was a glorious spectacle, and I was the only one there to enjoy it. The fire now reached the base of the cliff and then rushed up its sides. The squirrels ran before it in blind haste, and three pigeons dashed into the midst of the smoke. The flames flashed up the pines to their tops, as if they were powder.

When I found I was about to be surrounded by the fire, I retreated and joined the forces now arriving from the town. It took us several hours to surround the flames with our hoes and shovels and by back fires subdue them. In the midst of all I saw the farmer whom I first met, who had turned indifferently away saying it was none of his stuff, striving earnestly to save his corded wood, his stuff, which the fire had already seized and which it after all consumed.

It burned over a hundred acres or more and destroyed much young wood. When I returned home late in the day, with others of my towns-men, I could not help noticing that the crowd who were so ready to condemn the individual who had kindled the fire did not sympathize with the owners of the wood, but were in fact highly elate and as it were thankful for the opportunity which had afforded them so much sport; and it was only half a dozen owners, so called, though not all of them, who looked sour or grieved, and I felt that I had a deeper interest in the woods, knew them better and should feel their loss more, than any or all of them. The farmer whom I had first conducted to the woods was obliged to ask me the shortest way back, through his own lot. Why, then, should the half-dozen owners [and] the individuals who set the fire alone feel sorrow for the loss of the wood, while the rest of the town have their spirits raised? Some of the owners, however, bore their loss like men, but other some declared behind my back that I was a "damned rascal;" and a flibbertigibbet or two, who crowed like the old cock, shouted some reminiscences of "burnt woods" from safe recesses for some years after. I have had nothing to say to any of them. The locomo-tive engine has since burned over nearly all the same ground and more, and in some measure blotted out the memory of the previous fire. For a long time after I had learned this lesson I marvelled that while matches and tinder were contemporaries the world was not consumed; why the houses that have hearths were not burned before another day; if the flames were not as hungry now as when I waked them: I at once ceased to regard the owners and my own fault, — if fault there was any in the matter, — and attended to the phenomenon before me, determined to make the most of it. To be sure, I felt a little ashamed when I reflected on

what a trivial occasion this had happened, that at the time I was no better
employed than my townsmen.

That night I watched the fire, where some stumps still flamed at
midnight in the midst of the blackened waste, wandering through the
woods by myself; and far in the night I threaded my way to the spot
where the fire had taken, and discovered the now broiled fish, — which
had been dressed, — scattered over the burnt grass. . . .

[Undated, Long Island] . . . The oystermen had anchored their boat
near the shore without regard to the state of the tide, and when we came
to it to set sail, just after noon, we found that it was aground. Seeing that
they were preparing to push it off, I was about to take off my shoes and
stockings in order to wade to it first, but a Dutch sailor with a singular
bullfrog or trilobite expression of the eyes, whose eyes were like frog
ponds in the broad platter of his cheeks and gleamed like a pool covered
with frog-spittle, immediately offered me the use of his back. So mount-
ing, with my legs under his arms, and hugging him like one of [the]
family, he set me aboard of the periauger?

They then leaned their hardest against the stern, bracing their feet
against the sandy bottom in two feet of water, the Dutchman with his
broad back among them. In the most Dutch-like and easy way they
applied themselves to this labor, while the skipper tried to raise the
bows, never jerking or hustling but silently exerting what vigor was
inherent in them, doing, no doubt, their utmost endeavor, while I
pushed with a spike pole; but it was all in vain. It was decided to be
unsuccessful; we did not disturb its bed by a grain of sand. "Well, what
now?" said I. "How long have we got to wait?" "Till the tide rises," said
the captain. But no man knew of the tide, how it was. So I went in to
bathe, looking out for sharks and chasing crabs, and the Dutchman
waded out among the mussels to spear a crab. The skipper stuck a
clamshell into the sand at the water's edge to discover if it was rising, and
the sailors, — the Dutchman and the other, — having got more drink at
Oakes's, stretched themselves on the seaweed close to the water's edge
[and] went to sleep. After an hour or more we could discover no change
in the shell even by a hair's breadth, from which we learned that it was
about the turn of the tide and we must wait some hours longer. . . .

1851

Jan. 2. Saw at Clinton last night a room at the gingham-mills which covers one and seven-eighths acres and contains 578 looms, not to speak of spindles, both throttle and mule. The rooms all together cover three acres. They were using between three and four hundred horse-power, and kept an engine of two hundred horse-power, with a wheel twenty-three feet in diameter and a band ready to supply deficiencies, which have not often occurred. Some portion of the machinery — I think it was where the cotton was broken up, lightened up, and mixed before being matted together — revolved eighteen hundred times in a minute.

I first saw the pattern room where patterns are made by a hand loom. There were two styles of warps ready for the woof or filling. The operator must count the threads of the woof, which in the mill is done by the machinery. It was the ancient art of weaving, the shuttle flying back and forth, putting in the filling. As long as the warp is the same, it is but one "style," so called.

The cotton should possess a long staple and be clean and free from seed. The Sea Island cotton has a long staple and is valuable for thread. Many bales are thoroughly mixed to make the goods of one quality. The cotton is then torn to pieces and thoroughly lightened up by cylinders armed with hooks and by fans; then spread, a certain weight on a square yard, and matted together, and torn up and matted together again two or three times over; then the matted cotton fed to a cylindrical card, a very thin web of it, which is gathered into a copper trough, making six (the six-card machines) flat, rope-like bands, which are united into one at the railway head and drawn. And this operation of uniting and drawing or stretching goes on from one machine to another until the thread is spun, which is then dyed (calico is printed after being woven), — having been wound off on to reels and so made into skeins, — dyed and dried by steam; then, by machinery, wound on to spools for the warp and the woof. From a great many spools the warp is drawn off over cylinders and different-colored threads properly mixed and arranged. Then the ends of the warp are drawn through the harness of the loom by hand. The operator knows the succession of red, blue, green, etc., threads, having the numbers given her, and draws them through the harness accordingly, keeping count. Then the woof is put in, or it is *woven!!* Then the inequalities or nubs are picked off by girls. If *they* discover any imperfection, they tag it, and if necessary the wages of the weaver are reduced. Now, I think, it is passed over a red-hot iron cylinder, and the fuzz singed off, then washed with wheels with cold water; then the water forced out by centrifugal force within horizontal wheels. Then it is starched, the ends stitched together by machinery; then stretched smooth, dried, and ironed by machinery; then measured, folded, and packed.

This the agent, Forbes, says is the best gingham-mill in this country. The goods are better than the imported. The English have even stolen their name Lancaster Mills, calling them "Lancasterian."

The machinery is some of it peculiar, part of the throttle spindles (?) for instance.

The coach-lace-mill, only place in this country where it is made by machinery; made of thread of different materials, as cotton, worsted, linen, as well as colors, the raised figure produced by needles inserted woof fashion. Well worth examining further. Also pantaloon stuffs made in same mill and dyed after being woven, the woolen not taking the same dye with the cotton; hence a slight parti-colored appearance. These goods are sheared, *i. e.* a part of the nap taken off, making them smoother. Pressed between pasteboards.

The Brussels carpets made at the carpet-factory said to be the best in the world. Made like coach lace, only wider.

Erastus (?) Bigelow inventor of what is new in the above machinery; and, with his brother and another, owner of the carpet-factory.

I am struck by the fact that no work has been shirked when a piece of cloth is produced. Every thread has been counted in the finest web; it has not been matted together. The operator has succeeded only by patience, perseverance, and fidelity. . . .

July 16. Wednesday. Methinks my present experience is nothing; my past experience is all in all. I think that no experience which I have to-day comes up to, or is comparable with, the experiences of my boyhood. And not only this is true, but as far back as I can remember I have unconsciously referred to the experiences of a previous state of existence. "For life is a forgetting," etc. Formerly, methought, nature developed as I developed, and grew up with me. My life was ecstasy. In youth, before I lost any of my senses, I can remember that I was all alive, and inhabited my body with inexpressible satisfaction; both its weariness and its refreshment were sweet to me. This earth was the most glorious musical instrument, and I was audience to its strains. To have such sweet impressions made on us, such ecstasies begotten of the breezes! I can remember how I was astonished. I said to myself, — I said to others, — "There comes into my mind such an indescribable, infinite, all-absorbing, divine, heavenly pleasure, a sense of elevation and expansion, and [I] have had nought to do with it. I perceive that I am dealt with by superior powers. This is a pleasure, a joy, an existence which I have not procured myself. I speak as a witness on the stand, and tell what I have perceived." The morning and the evening were sweet to me, and I led a life aloof from society of men. I wondered if a mortal had ever known what I knew. I looked in books for some recognition of a kindred experience, but, strange to say, I found none. Indeed, I was slow to discover that other men had had this experience, for it had been possible to read books and to associate with men on other grounds. The maker of me was improving me. When I detected this interference I was profoundly moved. For years I marched as to a music in comparison with which the military music of the streets is noise and discord. I was daily intoxicated, and yet no man could call me intemperate. With all your science can you tell how it is, and whence it is, that light comes into the soul? . . .

Nov. 14. Friday. . . . In the evening went to a party. It is a bad place to go to, — thirty or forty persons, mostly young women, in a small room, warm and noisy. Was introduced to two young women. The first one was as lively and loquacious as a chickadee; had been accustomed to the society of watering-places, and therefore could get no refreshment out of such a dry fellow as I. The other was said to be pretty-looking, but I rarely look people in their faces, and, moreover, I could not hear what she said, there was such a clacking, — could only see the motion of her lips when I looked that way. I could imagine better places for conversation, where there should be a certain degree of silence surrounding you, and less than forty talking at once. Why, this afternoon, even, I did better. There was old Mr. Joseph Hosmer and I ate our luncheon of cracker and cheese together in the woods. I heard all he said, though it was not much, to be sure, and he could hear me. And then he talked out of such a glorious repose, taking a leisurely bite at the cracker and cheese between his words; and so some of him was communicated to me, and some of me to him, I trust.

These parties, I think, are a part of the machinery of modern society, that young people may be brought together to form marriage connections.

What is the use of going to see people whom yet you never see, and who never see you? I begin to suspect that it is not necessary that we should see one another.

Some of my friends make singular blunders. They go out of their way to talk with certain young women of whom they think, or have heard, that they are pretty, and take pains to introduce me to them. That may be a reason why they should look at them, but it is not a reason why they should talk with them. I confess that I am lacking a sense, perchance, in this respect, and I derive no pleasure from talking with a young woman half an hour simply because she has regular features. The society of young women is the most unprofitable I have ever tried. They are so light and flighty that you can never be sure whether they are there or not there. I prefer to talk with the more staid and settled, *settled for life*, in every sense. . . .

1852

Feb. 13. Talking with Rice this afternoon about the bees which I discovered the other day, he told me something about his bee-hunting. He and Pratt go out together once or twice a year. He takes a little tin box with a little refined sugar and water about the consistency of honey, or some honey in the comb, which comes up so high only in the box as to let the lid clear a bee's back, also some little bottles of paint — red, blue, white, etc. — and a compass properly prepared to line the bees with, the sights perhaps a foot apart. Then they ride off (this is in the fall) to some extensive wood, perhaps the west side of Sudbury. They go to some buckwheat-field or a particular species of late goldenrod which especially the bees frequent at that season, and they are sure to find honey-bees enough. They catch one by putting the box under the blossoms and then covering him with the lid, at the same time cutting off the stalk of the flower. They then set down the box, and after a while raise the lid slightly to see if the bee is feeding; if so, they take off the lid, knowing that he will not fly away till he gets ready, and catch another; and so on till they get a sufficient number. Then they thrust sticks into their little paint-bottles, and, with these, watching their opportunity, they give the bees each a spot of a particular color on his body, — they spot him distinctly, — and then, lying about a rod off, not to scare them, and watching them carefully all the while, they wait till one has filled his sac, and prepares to depart to his hive. They are careful to note whether he has a red or a blue jacket or what color. He rises up about ten feet and then begins to circle rapidly round and round with a hum, sometimes a circle twenty feet in diameter before he has decided which way to steer, and then suddenly shoots off in a bee-line to his hive. The hunters lie flat on their backs and watch him carefully all the while. If blue-jacket steers toward the open land where there are known to be hives, they forthwith leave out of the box all the blue-jackets, and move off a little and open the box in a new place to get rid of that family. And so they work till they come to a bee, red-jacket perhaps, that steers into the wood or swamp or in a direction to suit them.

They take the point of compass exactly, and wait perhaps till red-jacket comes back, that they may ascertain his course more exactly, and also judge by the time it has taken for him to go and return, using their watches, how far off the nest is, though sometimes they are disappointed in their calculations, for it may take the [bee] more or less time to crawl into its nest, depending on its position in the tree. By the third journey he will commonly bring some of his companions. Our hunters then move forward a piece, from time to time letting out a bee to make sure of their course. After the bees have gone and come once, they generally steer straight to their nest at once without circling round first. Sometimes the hunters, having observed this course carefully on the compass, go round a quarter of a circle and, letting out another bee, observe the course from that point, knowing that where these two lines intersect must be the nest. Rice thinks that a bee-line does not vary more than fifteen or twenty feet from a straight one in going half a mile. They frequently trace the bees thus to their hives more than a mile.

He said that the last time he went out the wind was so strong that the bees made some leeway just as a bullet will, and he could not get the exact course to their hives. He has a hive of bees over in Sudbury, and he every year sows some buckwheat for them. He has visited this buckwheat when in blossom when there was more than one bee to every six inches square, and out of curiosity has caught a number of the bees and, letting them out successively, has calculated by the several courses they took whose hives they came from in almost every instance, though some had come more than two miles and others belonged to his own hive close by.

He has seen a dozen hogsheads of honey from South America on the wharf at Boston. Says they manufacture honey now from maple syrup, which you cannot tell from bee honey, taking care to throw some dead bees and bees' wings and a little honeycomb into it.

He was repaid if he found the nest, even if he did not get any honey. I am glad to know that there are such grown children left. He says the mountain honeysuckle (columbine) has a good deal of honey at the bottom of the flower which the bee cannot get at in the usual way; it therefore gnaws a hole in it from the outside.

The actual bee-hunter and pigeon-catcher is familiar with facts in the natural history of bees and pigeons which Huber and even Audubon are totally ignorant of. I love best the unscientific man's knowledge; there is so much more humanity in it. It is connected with true *sports*. . . .

April 16. . . . As I turned round the corner of Hubbard's Grove, saw a woodchuck, the first of the season, in the middle of the field, six or seven rods from the fence which bounds the wood, and twenty rods distant. I ran along the fence and cut him off, or rather overtook him, though he started at the same time. When I was only a rod and a half off, he stopped, and I did the same; then he ran again, and I ran up within three feet of him, when he stopped again, the fence being between us. I squatted down and surveyed him at my leisure. His eyes were dull black and rather inobvious, with a faint chestnut (?) iris, with but little expression and that more of resignation than of anger. The general aspect was a coarse grayish brown, a sort of grisel (?). A lighter brown next the skin, then black or very dark brown and tipped with whitish rather loosely. The head between a squirrel and a bear, flat on the top and dark brown, and darker still or black on the tip of the nose. The whiskers black, two inches long. The ears very small and roundish, set far back and nearly buried in the fur. Black feet, with long and slender claws for digging. It appeared to tremble, or perchance shivered with cold. When I moved, it gritted its teeth quite loud, sometimes striking the under jaw against the other chatteringly, sometimes grinding one jaw on the other, yet as if more from instinct than anger. Whichever way I turned, that way it headed. I took a twig a foot long and touched its snout, at which it started forward and bit the stick, lessening the distance between us to two feet, and still it held all the ground it gained. I played with it tenderly awhile with the stick, trying to open its gritting jaws. Ever its long incisors, two above and two below, were presented. But I thought it would go to sleep if I stayed long enough. It did not sit upright as sometimes, but *standing* on its fore feet with its head down, *i. e.* half sitting, half standing. We sat looking at one another about half an hour, till we began to feel mesmeric influences. When I was tired, I moved away, wishing to see him run, but I could not start him. He would not stir as long as I was looking at him or could see him. I walked round him; he turned as fast and fronted me still. I sat down by his side within a foot. I talked to him *quasi* forest lingo, baby-talk, at any rate in a conciliatory tone, and thought that I had some influence on him. He gritted his teeth less. I chewed checkerberry leaves and presented them to his nose at last without a grit; though I saw that by so much gritting of the teeth he had worn them rapidly and they were covered with a fine white powder, which, if you measured it thus, would have made his anger terrible. He did not mind any noise I might make. With a little stick I lifted one of his paws to examine it, and held it up at pleasure. I turned him over to see what color he was beneath (darker or more purely brown), though he turned himself back again sooner than I could have wished. His tail was also all brown, though not very dark, rat-tail like, with loose hairs standing out on all sides like a caterpillar brush. He had a rather mild look. I spoke kindly to him. I reached checkerberry leaves to his mouth. I stretched my hands over him, though he turned up his head and still gritted a little. I laid my hand on him, but immediately took it off again, instinct not being wholly overcome. If I had had a few fresh bean leaves, thus in advance of the season, I am sure I should have tamed him completely. It was a frizzly tail. His is a humble, terrestrial color like the partridge's, well concealed where dead wiry grass rises above darker brown or chestnut dead leaves, — a modest color. If I had had some food, I should have ended with stroking him at my leisure. Could easily have wrapped him in my handkerchief. He was not fat nor particularly lean. I finally had to leave him without seeing him move from the place. A large, clumsy, burrowing squirrel. *Arctomys*, bear-mouse. I respect him as one of the natives. He lies there, by his color and habits so naturalized amid the dry leaves, the withered grass, and the bushes. A sound nap, too, he has enjoyed in his native fields, the past winter. I think I might learn some wisdom of him. His ancestors have lived here longer than mine. He is more thoroughly acclimated and naturalized than I. Bean leaves the red man raised for him, but he can do without them. . . .

1853

May 22. Sunday. . . . When yesterday Sophia and I were rowing past Mr. Prichard's land, where the river is bordered by a row of elms and low willows, at 6 P. M., we heard a singular note of distress as it were from a catbird — a loud, vibrating, catbird sort of note, as if the catbird's mew were imitated by a smart vibrating spring. Blackbirds and others were flitting about, apparently attracted by it. At first, thinking it was merely some peevish catbird or red-wing, I was disregarding it, but on second thought turned the bows to the shore, looking into the trees as well as over the shore, thinking some bird might be in distress, caught by a snake or in a forked twig. The hovering birds dispersed at my approach; the note of distress sounded louder and nearer as I approached the shore covered with low osiers. The sound came from the ground, not from the trees. I saw a little black animal making haste to meet the boat under the osiers. A young muskrat? a mink? No, it was a little dot of a kitten. It was scarcely six inches long from the face to the base — or I might as well say the tip — of the tail, for the latter was a short, sharp pyramid, perfectly perpendicular but not swelled in the least. It was a very handsome and very precocious kitten, in perfectly good condition, its breadth being considerably more than one third of its length. Leaving its mewing, it came scrambling over the stones as fast as its weak legs would permit, straight to me. I took it up and dropped it into the boat, but while I was pushing off it ran the length of the boat to Sophia, who held it while we rowed homeward. Evidently it had not been weaned — was smaller than we remembered that kittens ever were — almost infinitely small; yet it had hailed a boat, its life being in danger, and saved itself. Its performance, considering its age and amount of experience, was more wonderful than that of any young mathematician or musician that I have read of. Various were the conjectures as to how the kitten came there, a quarter of a mile from a house. The possible solutions were finally reduced to three: first, it must either have been born there, or, secondly, carried there by its mother, or, thirdly, by human hands. In the first case, it had possibly brothers and sisters, one or both, and its mother had left them to go a-hunting on her own account and might be expected back. In the second, she might equally be expected to return. At any rate, not having thought of all this till we got home, we found that we had got ourselves into a scrape; for this kitten, though exceedingly interesting, required one nurse to attend it constantly for the present, and, of course, another to spell the first; and, beside, we had already a cat well-nigh grown, who manifested such a disposition toward the young stranger that we had no doubt it would have torn it in pieces in a moment if left alone with it. As nobody made up his or her mind to have it drowned, and still less to drown it, — having once looked into its innocent extremely pale blue eyes (as of milk thrice skimmed) and had his finger or his chin sucked by it, while, its eyes being shut, its little paws played a soothing tune, — it was resolved to keep it till it could be suitably disposed of. It rested nowhere, in no lap, under no covert, but still faintly cried for its mother and its accustomed supper. It ran toward every sound or movement of a human being, and whoever crossed the room it was sure to follow at a rapid pace. It had all the ways of a cat of the maturest years; could purr divinely and raised its back to rub all boots and shoes. When it raised its foot to scratch its ear, which by the way it never hit, it was sure to fall over and roll on the floor. It climbed straight up the sitter, faintly mewing all the way, and sucked his chin. In vain, at first, its head was bent down into saucers of milk which its eyes did not see, and its chin was wetted. But soon it learned to suck a finger that had been dipped in it, and better still a rag; and then at last it slept and rested. The street was explored in vain to find its owner, and at length an Irish family took it into their cradle. Soon after we learned that a neighbor who had heard the mewing of kittens in the partition had sent for a carpenter, taken off a board, and found two the very day at noon that we sailed. That same hour it was first brought to the light a coarse Irish cook had volunteered to drown it, had carried it to the river, and without bag or sinker had cast it in! It saved itself and hailed a boat! What an eventful life! What a precocious kitten! We feared it owed its first plump condition to the water. How strong and effective the instinct of self-preservation! . . .

June 16. . . . Coming along near the celtis I heard a singular sound as of a bird in distress amid the bushes, and turned to relieve it. Next thought it a squirrel in an apple tree barking at me. Then found that it came from a hole in the ground under my feet, a loud sound between a grunting and a wheezing, yet not unlike the sound a red squirrel sometimes makes, but louder. Looking down the hole, I saw the tail and hind quarters of a woodchuck, which seemed to be contending with another further down. Reaching down carefully, I took hold of the tail, and, though I had to pull very hard indeed, I drew him out between the rocks, a bouncing great fat fellow, and tossed him a little way down the hill. As soon as he recovered from his bewilderment he made for the hole again, but, I barring the way, he ran off elsewhere. . . .

June 17. Friday. . . . Here have been three ultra-reformers, lecturers on Slavery, Temperance, the Church, etc., in and about our house and Mrs. Brooks's the last three or four days, — A. D. Foss, once a Baptist minister in Hopkinton, N. H.; Loring Moody, a sort of travelling pattern-working chaplain; and H. C. Wright, who shocks all the old women with his infidel writings. Though Foss was a stranger to the others, you would have thought them old and familiar cronies. (They happened here together by accident.) They addressed each other constantly by their Christian names, and rubbed you continually with the greasy cheeks of their kindness. They would not keep their distance, but cuddle up and lie spoon-fashion with you, no matter how hot the weather nor how narrow the bed, — chiefly ——. I was awfully pestered with his benignity; feared I should get greased all over with it past restoration; tried to keep some starch in my clothes. He wrote a book called "A Kiss for a Blow," and he behaved as if there were no alternative between these, or as if I had given him a blow. I would have preferred the blow, but he was bent on giving me the kiss, when there was neither quarrel nor agreement between us. I wanted that he should straighten his back, smooth out those ogling wrinkles of benignity about his eyes, and, with a healthy reserve, pronounce something in a downright manner. It was difficult to keep clear of his slimy benignity, with which he sought to cover you before he swallowed you and took you fairly into his bowels. It would have been far worse than the fate of Jonah. I do not wish to get any nearer to a man's bowels than usual. They lick you as a cow her calf. They would fain wrap you about with their bowels. —— addressed me as "Henry" within one minute from the time I first laid eyes on him, and when I spoke, he said with drawling, sultry sympathy, "Henry, I know all you would say; I understand you perfectly; you need not explain anything to me;" and to another, "I am going to dive into Henry's inmost depths." I said, "I trust you will not strike your head against the bottom." He could tell in a dark room, with his eyes blinded and in perfect stillness, if there was one there whom he loved. One of the most attractive things about the flowers is their beautiful reserve. The truly beautiful and noble puts its lover, as it were, at an infinite distance, while it attracts him more strongly than ever. I do not like the men who come so near me with their bowels. It is the most disagreeable kind of snare to be caught in. Men's bowels are far more slimy than their brains. They must be ascetics indeed who approach you by this side. What a relief to have heard the ring of one healthy reserved tone! With such a forgiving disposition, as if he were all the while forgiving you for existing. Considering our condition or *habit* of soul, — maybe corpulent and asthmatic, — maybe dying of atrophy, with all our bones sticking out, — is it kindness to embrace a man? They lay their sweaty hand on your shoulder, or your knee, to magnetize you. . . .

Oct. 12. To-day I have had the experience of borrowing money for a poor Irishman who wishes to get his family to this country. One will never know his neighbors till he has carried a subscription paper among them. Ah! it reveals many and sad facts to stand in this relation to them. To hear the selfish and cowardly excuses some make, — that *if* they help any they must help the Irishman who lives with them, — and him they are sure never to help! Others, with whom public opinion weighs, will think of it, trusting you never will raise the sum and so they will not be called on again; who give stingily after all. What a satire in the fact that you are much more inclined to call on a certain slighted and so-called crazy woman in moderate circumstances rather than on the president of the bank! But some are generous and save the town from the distinction which threatened it, and *some* even who do not lend, plainly would if they could.

Oct. 28. . . . For a year or two past, my *publisher*, falsely so called, has been writing from time to time to ask what disposition should be made of the copies of "A Week on the Concord and Merrimack Rivers" still on hand, and at last suggesting that he had use for the room they occupied in his cellar. So I had them all sent to me here, and they have arrived to-day by express, filling the man's wagon, — 706 copies out of an edition of 1000 which I bought of Munroe four years ago and have been ever since paying for, and have not quite paid for yet. The wares are sent to me at last, and I have an opportunity to examine my purchase. They are something more substantial than fame, as my back knows, which has borne them up two flights of stairs to a place similar to that to which they trace their origin. Of the remaining two hundred and ninety and odd, seventy-five were given away, the rest sold. I have now a library of nearly nine hundred volumes, over seven hundred of which I wrote myself. Is it not well that the author should behold the fruits of his labor? My works are piled up on one side of my chamber half as high as my head, my *opera omnia*. This is authorship; these are the work of my brain. There was just one piece of good luck in the venture. The unbound were tied up by the printer four years ago in stout paper wrappers, and inscribed, —

H. D. THOREAU'S
CONCORD RIVER
50 COPS.

So Munroe had only to cross out "River" and write "Mass." and deliver them to the expressman at once. I can see now what I write for, the result of my labors.

Nevertheless, in spite of this result, sitting beside the inert mass of my works, I take up my pen to-night to record what thought or experience I may have had, with as much satisfaction as ever. Indeed, I believe that this result is more inspiring and better for me than if a thousand had bought my wares. It affects my privacy less and leaves me freer.

Dec. 8. . . . I was amused by R. W. E.'s telling me that he drove his own calf out of the yard, as it was coming in with the cow, not knowing it to be his own, a drove going by at the time.

1854

Feb. 12. . . . P. M. — Skate to Pantry Brook.

Put on skates at mouth of Swamp Bridge Brook. The ice appears to be nearly two inches thick. There are many rough places where the crystals are very coarse, and the old ice on the river (for I spoke of a new ice since the freshet) is uneven and covered, more or less, with the scales of a thin ice whose water is dried up. In some places, where the wind has been strong, the foam is frozen into great concentric ridges, over which with an impetus I dash. It is hobbling and tearing work.

Just beyond the bathing-place, I see the wreck of an ice-fleet, which yesterday morning must have been very handsome. It reminds me of a vast and crowded fleet of sloops with large slanting sails all standing to the north. These sails are, some of them, the largest specimens of the leaf-structure in ice that I have seen, eight or nine inches long. Perhaps this structure is more apparent now they have wasted so much. Their bases can be seen continuing quite through the level ice which has formed about them, as if the wind and waves, breaking up a thin ice, had held it in that position while it froze in.

One accustomed to glide over a boundless and variegated ice floor like this cannot be much attracted by tessellated floors and mosaic work. I skate over a thin ice all tessellated, so to speak, or in which you see the forms of the crystals as they shot. This is separated by two or three feet of water from the old ice resting on the meadow. The water, consequently, is not dark, as when seen against a muddy bottom, but a clear yellow, against which the white air-bubbles in and under the ice are very conspicuous.

Landed at Fair Haven Hill. I was not aware till I came out how pleasant a day it was. It was very cold this morning, and I have been putting [on] wood in vain to warm my chamber, and lo! I come forth, and am surprised to find it warm and pleasant. There is very little wind, here under Fair Haven especially. I begin to dream of summer even. I take off my mittens.

Here is a little hollow which, for a short time every spring, gives passage to the melting snow, and it was consequently wet there late into the spring. I remember well when a few little alder bushes, encouraged by the moisture, first sprang up in it. They now make a perfect little grove, fifteen feet high, and maybe half a dozen rods long, with a rounded outline, as if they were one mass of moss, with the wrecks of ferns in their midst and the sweet-fern about its edge. And so, perchance, a swamp is beginning to be formed. The shade and the decaying vegetation may at last produce a spongy soil, which will supply a constant rill. Has not something like this been the history of the alder swamp and brook a little further along? True, the first is on a small scale and rather elevated, part way up the hill; and ere long trout begin to glance in the brook, where first was merely a course for melted snow which turned the dead grass-blades all one way, — which combed the grassy tresses down the hill.

This is a glorious winter afternoon. The clearness of a winter day is not impaired, while the air is still and you feel a direct heat from the sun. It is not like the relenting of a thaw with a southerly wind. There is a bright sheen from the snow, and the ice booms a little from time to time. On those parts of the hill which are bare, I see the radical leaves of the buttercup, mouse-ear, and the thistle.

Especially do gray rocks or cliffs with a southwest exposure attract us now, where there is warmth and dryness. The gray color is nowhere else so agreeable to us as in these rocks in the sun at this season, where I hear the trickling of water under great ice organ-pipes.

What a floor it is I glide thus swiftly over! It is a study for the slowest walker. See the shells of countless air-bubbles within and beneath it, some a yard or two in diameter. Beneath they are crowded together from the size of a dollar downward. They give the ice a white-spotted or freckled appearance. Specimens of every coin (*numismata*) from the first minting downward. I hear the pond faintly boom or mutter in a low voice, promising another spring to the fishes. I saw yesterday deeply scalloped oak leaves which had sunk nearly an inch into the ice of Walden, making a perfect impression of their forms, on account of the heat they absorbed. Their route is thus downward to dust again, through water and snow and ice and every obstacle. This thin meadow ice with yellow water under it yields a remarkable hollow sound, like a drum, as I rip over it, as if it were about to give way under me, — some of that gong-like roar which I have described elsewhere, — the ice being tense. I crossed the road at Bidens Brook. Here the smooth ice was dusty (from the road) a great distance, and I thought it would dull my skates.

To make a perfect winter day like this, you must have a clear, spar-kling air, with a sheen from the snow, sufficient cold, little or no wind; and the warmth must come directly from the sun. It must not be a thawing warmth. The tension of nature must not be relaxed. The earth must be resonant if bare, and you hear the lisping tinkle of chickadees from time to time and the unrelenting steel-cold scream of a jay, unmelted, that never flows into a song, a sort of wintry trumpet, scream-ing cold; hard, tense, frozen music, like the winter sky itself; in the blue livery of winter's band. It is like a flourish of trumpets to the winter sky. There is no hint of incubation in the jay's scream. Like the creak of a cart-wheel. There is no cushion for sounds now. They tear our ears.

Nov. 5. Sunday. To White Pond with Charles Wheeler.

Passing the mouth of John Hosmer's hollow near the river, was hailed by him and Anthony Wright, sitting there, to come and see where they had dug for money. There was a hole six feet square and as many deep, and the sand was heaped about over a rod square. Hosmer said that it was dug two or three weeks before, that three men came in a chaise and dug it in the night. They were seen about there by day. Somebody dug near there in June, and then they covered up the hole again. He said they had been digging thereabouts from time to time for a hundred years. I asked him why. He said that Dr. Lee, who lived where Joe Barrett did, told him that old Mr. Wood, who lived in a house very near his (Hosmer's), told him that, one night in Captain Kidd's day, three pirates came to his house with a pair of old-fashioned deer-skin breeches, both legs full of coin, and asked leave to bury it in his cellar. He was afraid, and refused them. They then asked for some earthen pots and shovels and a lanthorn, which he let them have. A woman in the house followed the pirates at a distance down the next hollow on the south, and saw them go along the meadow-side and turn up this hollow, and then, being alone and afraid, she returned. Soon after the men returned with the tools and an old-fashioned hat full of the coin (holding about a quart), which they gave to Wood. He, being afraid, buried it in his cellar, but afterward, becoming a poor man, dug it up and used it. A bailiff made some inquiry hereabouts after the pirates.

Hosmer said that one thing which confirmed the diggers in their belief was the fact that when he was a little boy, plowing one day with his father on the hillside, they found three old-fashioned bottles bottom upward but empty under the plow. Somebody consulted Moll Pitcher, who directed to dig at a certain distance from an apple tree on a line with the bottles, and then they would find the treasure. . . .

1855

March 22. . . . Going [along] the steep side-hill on the south of the pond about 4 P. M., on the edge of the little patch of wood which the choppers have not yet levelled, — though they have felled many an acre around it this winter, — I observed a rotten and hollow hemlock stump about two feet high and six inches in diameter, and instinctively approached with my right hand ready to cover it. I found a flying squirrel in it, which, as my left hand had covered a small hole at the bottom, ran directly into my right hand. It struggled and bit not a little, but my cotton glove protected me, and I felt its teeth only once or twice. It also uttered three or four dry shrieks at first, something like *cr-r-rack cr-r-r-ack cr-r-r-ack.* I rolled it up in my handkerchief and, holding the ends tight, carried it home in my hand, some three miles. It struggled more or less all the way, especially when my feet made any unusual or louder noise going through leaves or bushes. I could count its claws as they appeared through the handkerchief, and once it got its head out a hole. It even bit through the handkerchief.

Color, as I remember, above a chestnut ash, inclining to fawn or cream color (?), slightly browned; beneath white, the under edge of its wings (?) tinged yellow, the upper dark, perhaps black, making a dark stripe. Audubon and Bachman do not speak of any such stripe! It was a very cunning little animal, reminding me of a mouse in the room. Its very large and prominent black eyes gave it an interesting innocent look. Its very neat flat, fawn-colored, distichous tail was a great ornament. Its "sails" were not very obvious when it was at rest, merely giving it a flat appearance beneath. It would leap off and upward into the air two or three feet from a table, spreading its "sails," and fall to the floor in vain; perhaps strike the side of the room in its upward spring and endeavor to cling to it. It would run up the window by the sash, but evidently found the furniture and walls and floor too hard and smooth for it and after some falls became quiet. In a few moments it allowed me to stroke it, though far from confident.

I put it in a barrel and covered it for the night. It was quite busy all the evening gnawing out, clinging for this purpose and gnawing at the upper edge of a sound oak barrel, and then dropping to rest from time to time. It had defaced the barrel considerably by morning, and would probably have escaped if I had not placed a piece of iron against the gnawed part. I had left in the barrel some bread, apple, shagbarks, and cheese. It ate some of the apple and one shagbark, cutting it quite in two transversely.

In the morning it was quiet, and *squatted* somewhat curled up amid the straw, with its tail passing under it and the end curled over its head very prettily, as if to shield it from the light and keep it warm. I always found it in this position by day when I raised the lid.

March 23. P. M. — To Fair Haven Pond.

Carried my flying squirrel back to the woods in my handkerchief. I placed it, about 3.30 P. M., on the very stump I had taken it from. It immediately ran about a rod over the leaves and up a slender maple sapling about ten feet, then after a moment's pause sprang off and skimmed downward toward a large maple nine feet distant, whose trunk it struck three or four feet from the ground. This it rapidly ascended, on the opposite side from me, nearly thirty feet, and there clung to the main stem with its head downward, eying me. After two or three minutes' pause I saw that it was preparing for another spring by raising its head and looking off, and away it went in admirable style, more like a bird than any quadruped I had dreamed of and far surpassing the impression I had received from naturalists' accounts. I marked the spot it started from and the place where it struck, and measured the height and distance carefully. It sprang off from the maple at the height of twenty-eight and a half feet, and struck the ground at the foot of a tree fifty and a half feet distant, measured horizontally. Its flight was not a *regular* descent; it varied from a direct line both horizontally and vertically. Indeed it skimmed much like a hawk and part of its flight was nearly horizontal, and it diverged from a right line eight or ten feet to the right, making a curve in that direction. There were six trees from six inches to a foot in diameter, one a hemlock, in a direct line between the two termini, and these it skimmed partly round, and passed through their thinner limbs; did not as I could perceive touch a twig. It skimmed its way like a hawk between and around the trees. Though it was a windy day, this was on a steep hillside away from the wind and covered with wood, so it was not aided by that. As the ground rose about two feet, the distance was to the absolute height as fifty and a half to twenty-six and a half, or it advanced about two feet for every one foot of descent. After its vain attempts in the house, I was not prepared for this exhibition. It did not fall heavily as in the house, but struck the ground gently enough, and I cannot believe that the mere extension of the skin enabled it to skim so far. It must be still further aided by its organization. Perhaps it fills itself with air first. Perhaps I had a fairer view than common of its flight, now at 3.30 P. M. Audubon and Bachman say *he* saw it skim "about fifty yards," curving upwards at the end and alighting on the trunk of a tree. This in a meadow in which were scattered oaks and beeches. This near Philadelphia. Wesson [?] says he has seen them fly five or six rods.

Kicking over the hemlock stump, which was a mere shell with holes below, and a poor refuge, I was surprised to find a little nest at the bottom, open above just like a bird's nest, a mere bed. It was composed of leaves, shreds of bark, and dead pine-needles. As I remember, it was not more than an inch and a half broad when at rest, but when skimming through the air I should say it was four inches broad. This is the impression I now have. Captain John Smith says it is said to fly thirty or forty yards. Audubon and Bachman quote one Gideon B. Smith, M. D., of Baltimore, who has had much to do with these squirrels and speaks of their curving upward at the end of their flight to alight on a tree-trunk and of their "flying" into his windows. In order to perform all these flights, — to strike a tree at such a distance, etc., etc., — it is evident it must be able to steer. I should say that mine steered as a hawk that moves without flapping its wings, never being able, however, to get a new impetus after the first spring. . . .

April 15. 9 A. M. — To Atkins's boat-house.

No sun till setting. Another still, moist, overcast day, without sun, but all day a crescent of light, as if breaking away in the north. The waters smooth and full of reflections. A still cloudy day like this is perhaps the best to be on the water. To the clouds, perhaps, we owe both the stillness and the reflections, for the light is in great measure reflected from the water. Robins sing now at 10 A. M. as in the morning, and the phœbe; and pigeon woodpecker's cackle is heard, and many martins (with white-bellied swallows) are skimming and twittering above the water, perhaps catching the small fuzzy gnats with which the air is filled. The sound of church bells, at various distances, in Concord and the neighboring towns, sounds very sweet to us on the water this still day. It is the song of the villages heard with the song of the birds.

The Great Meadows are covered, except a small island in their midst, but not a duck do we see there. On a low limb of a maple on the edge of the river, thirty rods from the present shore, we saw a fish hawk eating a fish. Sixty rods off we could [see] his white crest. We landed, and got nearer by stealing through the woods. His legs looked long as he stood up on the limb with his back to us, and his body looked black against the sky and by contrast with the white of his head. There was a dark stripe on the side of the head. He had got the fish under his feet on the limb, and would bow his head, snatch a mouthful, and then look hastily over his right shoulder in our direction, then snatch another mouthful and look over his left shoulder. At length he launched off and flapped heavily away. We found at the bottom of the water beneath where he sat numerous fragments of the fish he had been eating, parts of the fins, entrails, gills, etc., and some was dropped on the bough. From one fin which I examined, I judged that it was either a sucker or a pout. There were small leeches adhering to it.

In the meanwhile, as we were stealing through the woods, we heard the pleasing note of the pine warbler, bringing back warmer weather, and we heard one honk of a goose, and, looking up, saw a large narrow harrow of them steering northeast. Half a mile further we saw another fish hawk, upon a dead limb midway up a swamp white oak over the water, at the end of a small island. We paddled directly toward him till within thirty rods. A crow came scolding to the tree and lit within three feet, looking about as large, compared with the hawk, as a crow blackbird to a crow, but he paid no attention to him. We had a very good view of him, as he sat sidewise to us, and of his eagle-shaped head and beak. The white feathers of his head, which were erected somewhat, made him look like a copple-crowned hen. When he launched off, he uttered a clear whistling note, — *phe phe, phe phe, phe phe,* — *somewhat* like that of a telltale, but more round and less shrill and rapid, and another, perhaps his mate, fifty rods off, joined him. They flew heavily, as we looked at them from behind, more like a blue heron and bittern than I was aware of, their long wings undulating slowly to the tip, like the heron's, and the bodies seeming sharp like a gull's and unlike a hawk's.

In the water beneath where he was perched, we found many fragments of a pout, — bits of red gills, entrails, fins, and some of the long flexible black feelers, — scattered for four or five feet. This pout appeared to have been quite fresh, and was probably caught alive. We afterward started one of them from an oak over the water a mile beyond, just above the boathouse, and he skimmed off very low over the water, several times striking it with a loud sound heard plainly sixty rods off at least; and we followed him with our eyes till we could only see faintly his undulating wings against the sky in the western horizon. You could probably tell if any were about by looking for fragments of fish under the trees on which they would perch.

We had scared up but few ducks — some apparently black, which quacked — and some small rolling-pins, probably teal.

Returning, we had a fine view of a blue heron, standing erect and open to view on a meadow island, by the great swamp south of the bridge, looking as broad as a boy on the side, and then some sheldrakes sailing in the smooth water beyond. These soon sailed behind points of meadow. The heron flew away, and one male sheldrake flew past us low over the water, reconnoitring, large and brilliant black and white. When the heron takes to flight, what a change in size and appearance! It is *presto change!* There go two great undulating wings pinned together, but the body and neck must have been left behind somewhere.

Before we rounded Ball's Hill, — the water now beautifully smooth, — at 2.30 P. M., we saw three gulls sailing on the glassy meadow at least half a mile off, by the oak peninsula, — the plainer because they were against the reflection of the hills. They looked larger than afterward close at hand, as if their whiteness was reflected and doubled. As we advanced into the Great Meadows, making the only ripples in their broad expanse, there being still not a ray of sunshine, only a subdued light through the thinner crescent in the north, the reflections of the maples, of Ponkawtasset and the poplar hill, and the whole township in the southwest, were as perfect as I ever saw. A wall which ran down to the water on the hillside, without any remarkable curve in it, was exaggerated by the reflection into the half of an ellipse. The meadow was expanded to a large lake, the shore-line being referred to the sides of the hills reflected in it. It was a scene worth many such voyages to see. It was remarkable how much light those white gulls, and also a bleached post on a distant shore, absorbed and reflected through that sombre atmosphere, — conspicuous almost as candles in the night. When we got near to the gulls, they rose heavily and flapped away, answering a more distant one, with a remarkable, deliberate, melancholy, squeaking scream, mewing, or piping, almost a squeal. It was a *little* like the loon. Is this sound the origin of the name sea-mew? Notwithstanding the smoothness of the water, we could not easily see black ducks against the reflection of the woods, but heard them rise at a distance before we saw them. The birds were still in the middle of the day, but began to sing again by 4.30 P. M., probably because of the clouds. Saw and heard a kingfisher — do they not come with the smooth waters of April? — hurrying over the meadow as if on urgent business. . . .

June 14. Thursday. . . . Looked at the peetweet's nest which C. found yesterday. It was very difficult to find again in the broad open meadow; no nest but a mere hollow in the dead cranberry leaves, the grass and stubble ruins, under a little alder. The old bird went off at last from under us; low in the grass at first and with *wings up*, making a worried sound which attracted other birds. I frequently noticed others afterward flying low over the meadow and alighting and uttering this same note of alarm. There [were] only four eggs in this nest yesterday, and to-day, to C.'s surprise, there are the two eggs which he left and a young peetweet beside; a gray pinch of down with a black centre to its back, but already so old and precocious that it runs with its long legs swiftly off from squatting beside the two eggs, and hides in the grass. We have some trouble to catch it. How came it here with these eggs, which will not be hatched for some days? C. saw nothing of it yesterday. J. Farmer says that young peetweets run at once like partridges and quails, and that they are the only birds he knows that do. These eggs were not addled (I had opened one, C. another). Did this bird come from another nest, or did it belong to an earlier brood? Eggs white, with black spots here and there all over, dim at great end.

A cherry-bird's nest and two eggs in an apple tree fourteen feet from ground. One egg, round black spots and a few oblong, about equally but thinly dispersed over the whole, and a dim, internal, purplish tinge about the large end. It is difficult to see anything of the bird, for she steals away early, and you may neither see nor hear anything of her while examining the nest, and so think it deserted. Approach very warily and look out for them a dozen or more rods off.

It suddenly began to rain with great violence, and we in haste drew up our boat on the Clamshell shore, upset it, and got under, sitting on the paddles, and so were quite dry while our friends thought we were being wet to our skins. But we had as good a roof as they. It was very pleasant to lie there half an hour close to the edge of the water and see and hear the great drops patter on the river, each making a great bubble; the rain seemed much heavier for it. The swallows at once and numerously began to fly low over the water in the rain, as they had not before, and the toads' spray rang in it. After it began to hold up, the wind veered a little to the east and apparently blew back the rear of the cloud, and blew a second rain somewhat in upon us.

As soon as the rain was over I crawled out, straightened my legs, and stumbled at once upon a little patch of strawberries within a rod, — the sward red with them. These we plucked while the last drops were thinly falling.

1856

Jan. 7. . . . They tell how I swung on a gown [?] on the stairway when I was at Chelmsford. The gown [?] gave way; I fell and fainted, and it took two pails of water to bring me to, for I was remarkable for holding my breath in those cases.

Mother tried to milk the cow which Father took on trial, but she kicked at her and spilt the milk. (They say a dog had bitten her teats.) Proctor laughed at her as a city girl, and then he tried, but the cow kicked him over, and he finished by beating her with his cowhide shoe. Captain Richardson milked her warily, standing up. Father came home, and thought he would "brustle right up to her," for she needed much to be milked, but suddenly she lifted her leg and "struck him fair and square right in the muns," knocked him flat, and broke the bridge of his nose, which shows it yet. He distinctly heard her hoof rattle on his nose. This "started the claret," and, without stanching the blood, he at once drove her home to the man he had her of. She ran at some young women by the way, who saved themselves by getting over the wall in haste.

Father complained of the powder in the meeting-house garret at town meeting, but it did not get moved while we lived there. Here he painted over his old signs for guide-boards, and got a fall when painting Hale's (?) factory. Here the bladder John was playing with burst on the hearth.

The cow came into the entry after pumpkins. I cut my toe, and was knocked over by a hen with chickens, etc., etc.

Mother tells how, at the brick house, we each had a little garden a few feet square, and I came in one day, having found a potato just sprouted, which by her advice I planted in my garden. Ere long John came in with a potato which he had found and had it planted in his garden, — "Oh, mother, I have found a potato all sprouted. I mean to put it in my garden," etc. Even Helen is said to have found one. But next I came crying that somebody had got my potato, etc., etc., but it was restored to me as the youngest and original discoverer, if not inventor, of the potato, and it grew in *my* garden, and finally its crop was dug by myself and yielded a dinner for the family.

I was kicked down by a passing ox. Had a chicken given me by Lidy — Hannah — and peeped through the keyhole at it. Caught an eel with John. Went to bed with new boots on, and after with cap. "Rasselas" given me, etc., etc. Asked P. Wheeler, "Who owns all the land?" Asked Mother, having got the medal for geography, "Is Boston in Concord?" If I had gone to Miss Wheeler a little longer, should have received the chief prize book, "Henry Lord Mayor," etc., etc. . . .

Feb. 28. . . . Our young maltese cat Min, which has been absent five cold nights, the ground covered deep with crusted snow, — her first absence, — and given up for dead, has at length returned at daylight, awakening the whole house with her mewing and afraid of the strange girl we have got in the meanwhile. She is a mere wrack of skin and bones, with a sharp nose and wiry tail. She is as one returned from the dead. There is as much rejoicing as at the return of the prodigal son, and if we had a fatted calf we should kill it. Various are the conjectures as to her adventures, — whether she has had a fit, been shut up somewhere, or lost, torn in pieces by a certain terrier or frozen to death. In the meanwhile she is fed with the best that the house affords, minced meats and saucers of warmed milk, and, with the aid of unstinted sleep in all laps in succession, is fast picking up her crumbs. She has already found her old place under the stove, and is preparing to make a stew of her brains there.

March 19. . . . WHAT BEFELL AT MRS. BROOKS'S. On the morning of the 17th, Mrs. Brooks's Irish girl Joan fell down the cellar stairs, and was found by her mistress lying at the bottom, apparently lifeless. Mrs. Brooks ran to the street-door for aid to get her up, and asked a Miss Farmer, who was passing, to call the blacksmith near by. The latter lady

turned instantly, and, making haste across the road on this errand, fell
flat in a puddle of melted snow, and came back to Mrs. Brooks's,
bruised and dripping and asking for opodeldoc. Mrs. Brooks again ran
to the door and called to George Bigelow to complete the unfinished
errand. He ran nimbly about it and fell flat in another puddle near the
former, but, his joints being limber, got along without opodeldoc and
raised the blacksmith. He also notified James Burke, who was passing,
and he, rushing in to render aid, fell off one side of the cellar stairs in
the dark. They no sooner got the girl up-stairs than she came to and
went raving, then had a fit.

Haste makes waste. It never rains but it pours. I have this from those
who have heard Mrs. Brooks's story, seen the girl, the stairs, and the
puddles. . . .

April 30. . . . People are talking about my Uncle Charles. Minott tells
how he heard Tilly Brown once asking him to show him a peculiar
(inside?) lock in wrestling. "Now, don't hurt me, don't throw me hard."
He struck his antagonist inside his knees with his feet, and so deprived
him of his legs. Hosmer remembers his tricks in the barroom, shuffling
cards, etc. He could do anything with cards, yet he did not gamble. He
would toss up his hat, twirling it over and over, and catch it on his head
invariably. Once wanted to live at Hosmer's, but the latter was afraid of
him. "Can't we study up something?" he asked. H. asked him into the
house and brought out apples and cider, and Charles talked. "You!" said
he, "I burst the bully of Lowell" (or Haverhill?). He wanted to wrestle;
would not be put off. "Well, we won't wrestle in the house." So they went
out to the yard, and a crowd got round. "Come spread some straw here,"
said C. "I don't want to hurt him." He threw him at once. They tried
again. He told them to spread more straw and he "burst" him.

He had a strong head and never got drunk; would drink gin sometimes, but not to excess. Did not use tobacco, except snuff out of
another's box sometimes. Was very neat in his person. Was not profane,
though vulgar. . . .

Uncle Charles used to say that he had n't a single tooth in his head.
The fact was they were all double, and I have heard that he lost about all
of them by the time he was twenty-one. Ever since I knew him he could
swallow his nose. . . .

Aug. 8. . . . 3.30 P. M. — When I came forth, thinking to empty my boat
and go a-meditating along the river, — for the full ditches and drenched

grass forbade other routes, except the highway, — and this is one advantage of a boat, — I learned to my chagrin that Father's pig was gone. He had leaped out of the pen some time since his breakfast, but his dinner was untouched. Here was an ugly duty not to be shirked, — a wild shoat that weighed but ninety to be tracked, caught, and penned, — an afternoon's work, at least (if I were lucky enough to accomplish it so soon), prepared for me, quite different from what I had anticipated. I felt chagrined, it is true, but I could not ignore the fact nor shirk the duty that lay so near to me. Do the duty that lies nearest to thee. I proposed to Father to sell the pig as he was running (somewhere) to a neighbor who had talked of buying him, making a considerable reduction. But my suggestion was not acted on, and the responsibilities of the case all devolved on me, for I could run faster than Father. Father looked to me, and I ceased to look to the river. Well, let us see if we can track him. Yes, this is the corner where he got out, making a step of his trough. Thanks to the rain, his tracks are quite distinct. Here he went along the edge of the garden over the water and muskmelons, then through the beans and potatoes, and even along the front-yard walk I detect the print of his divided hoof, his two sharp toes (*ungulæ*). It's a wonder we did not see him. And here he passed out under the gate, across the road, — how naked he must have felt! — into a grassy ditch, and whither next? Is it of any use to go hunting him up unless you have devised some mode of catching him when you have found? Of what avail to know where he has been, even where he is? He was so shy the little while we had him, of course he will never come back; he cannot be tempted by a swill-pail. Who knows how many miles off he is! Perhaps he has taken the back track and gone to Brighton, or Ohio! At most, probably we shall only have the satisfaction of glimpsing the nimble beast at a distance, from time to time, as he trots swiftly through the green meadows and cornfields. But, now I speak, what is that I see pacing deliberately up the middle of the street forty rods off? It is *he*. As if to tantalize, to tempt us to waste our afternoon without further hesitation, he thus offers himself. He roots a foot or two and then lies down on his belly in the middle of the street. But think not to catch him a-napping. He has his eyes about, and his ears too. He has already been chased. He gives that wagon a wide berth, and now, seeing me, he turns and trots back down the street. He turns into a front yard. Now if I can only close that gate upon him ninety-nine hundredths of the work is done, but ah! he hears me coming afar off, he foresees the danger, and, with swinish cunning and speed, he scampers out. My neighbor in the street tries to head him; he jumps to this side the road, then to that, before him; but the third time the pig was there first and went by. "Whose is it?" he shouts. "It's ours." He bolts into that neighbor's yard and so across his premises. He has been twice there before, it seems; he knows the road; see what work he has made in his flower-garden! He must be fond of bulbs. Our neighbor picks up one tall flower with its bulb attached, holds it out at arm's length. He is excited about the pig; it is a subject he is interested in. But where is [he] gone now? The last glimpse I had of him was as he went through the cow-yard; here are his tracks again in this corn-field, but they are lost in the grass. We lose him; we beat the bushes in vain; he may be far away. But hark! I heard a grunt. Nevertheless for half an hour I do not see him that grunted. At last I find fresh tracks along the river, and again lose them. Each neighbor whose garden I traverse tells me some anecdote of losing pigs, or the attempt to drive them, by which I am not encouraged. Once more he crosses our first neighbor's garden and is said to be in the road. But I am not there yet; it is a good way off. At length my eyes rest on him again, after three quarters of an hour's separation. There he trots with the whole road to himself, and now again drops on his belly in a puddle. Now he starts again, seeing me twenty rods [off], deliberates, considers which way I want him to go, and goes the other. There was some chance of driving him along the sidewalk, or letting him go rather, till he slipped under our gate again, but of what avail would that be? How corner and catch him who keeps twenty rods off? He never lets the open side of the triangle be less than half a dozen rods wide. There was one place where a narrower street turned off at right angles with the main one, just this side our yard, but I could not drive him past that. Twice he ran up the narrow street, for he knew I did not wish it, but though the main street was broad and open and no traveller in sight, when I tried to drive him past this opening he invariably turned his piggish head toward me, dodged from side to side, and finally ran up the narrow street or down the main one, as if there were a high barrier erected before him. But really he is no more obstinate than I. I cannot but respect his tactics and his independence. He will be he, and I may be I. He is not unreasonable because he thwarts me, but only the more reasonable. He has a strong will. He stands upon his idea. There is a wall across the path not where a man bars the way, but where he is resolved not to travel. Is he not superior to man therein? Once more he glides down the narrow street, deliberates at a corner, chooses wisely for him, and disappears through an openwork fence eastward. He has gone to fresh gardens and pastures new. Other neighbors stand in the doorways but half sympathizing, only observing, "Ugly thing to catch." "You have a job on your hands." I lose sight of him, but hear that he is far ahead in a large field. And there we try to let him alone a while, giving him a wide berth.

At this stage an Irishman was engaged to assist. "I can catch him," says he, with Buonapartean confidence. He thinks him a family Irish pig. His wife is with him, bareheaded, and his little flibbertigibbet of a boy, seven years old. "Here, Johnny, do you run right off there" (at the broadest possible angle with his own course). "Oh, but he can't do anything." "Oh, but I only want him to tell me where he is, — to keep sight of him." Michael soon discovers that he is not an Irish pig, and his wife and Johnny's occupation are soon gone. Ten minutes afterward I am patiently tracking him step by step through a corn-field, a near-sighted man helping me, and then into garden after garden far eastward, and finally into the highway, at the graveyard; but hear and see nothing. One suggests a dog to track him. Father is meanwhile selling him to the blacksmith, who also is trying to get sight of him. After fifteen minutes since he disappeared eastward, I hear that he has been to the river twice far on [?] the north, through the first neighbor's premises. I wend that way. He crosses the street far ahead, Michael behind; he dodges up an avenue. I stand in the gap there, Michael at the other end, and now he tries to corner him. But it is a vain hope to corner him in a yard. I see a carriage-manufactory door open. "Let him go in there, Flannery." For once the pig and I are of one mind; he bolts in, and the door is closed. Now for a rope. It is a large barn, crowded with carriages. The rope is at length obtained; the windows are barred with carriages lest he bolt through. He is resting quietly on his belly in the further corner, thinking unutterable things.

Now the course recommences within narrower limits. Bump, bump, bump he goes, against wheels and shafts. We get no hold yet. He is all ear and eye. Small boys are sent under the carriages to drive him out. He froths at the mouth and deters them. At length he is stuck for an instant between the spokes of a wheel, and I am securely attached to his hind leg. He squeals deafeningly, and is silent. The rope is attached to a hind leg. The door is opened, and the *driving* commences. Roll an egg as well. You may drag him, but you cannot drive him. But he is in the road, and now another thunder-shower greets us. I leave Michael with the rope in one hand and a switch in the other and go home. He seems to be gaining a little westward. But, after long delay, I look out and find that he makes but doubtful progress. A boy is made to face him with a stick, and it is only when the pig springs at him savagely that progress is made homeward. He will be killed before he is driven home. I get a wheelbarrow and go to the rescue. Michael is alarmed. The pig is rabid, snaps at him. We drag him across the barrow, hold him down, and so, at last, get him home.

If a wild shoat like this gets loose, first track him if you can, or otherwise discover where he is. Do not scare him more than you can help. Think of some yard or building or other inclosure that will hold him and, by showing your forces — yet as if uninterested parties — fifteen or twenty rods off, let him of his own accord enter it. Then slightly shut the gate. Now corner and tie him and put him into a cart or barrow.

All progress in driving at last was made by facing and endeavoring to switch him from home. He rushed upon you and made a few feet in the desired direction. When I approached with the barrow he advanced to meet it with determination.

So I get home at dark, wet through and supperless, covered with mud and wheel-grease, without any rare flowers. . . .

Aug. 26. Tuesday. . . . Last Friday (the 22d) afternoon (when I was away), Father's pig got out again and took to the riverside. The next day he was heard from, but not found. That night he was seen on an island in the meadow, in the midst of the flood, but thereafter for some time no account of him. J. Farmer advised to go to Ai Hale, just over the Carlisle line. He has got a dog which, if you put him on the track of the pig not more than four hours' old, will pursue and catch him and hold him by the ear without hurting him till you come up. That's the best way. Ten men cannot stop him in the road, but he will go by them. It was generally conceded that the right kind of dog was all that was wanted, like Ai Hale's, one that would hold him by the ear, but not uselessly maim him. One or two said, "If I only had such a one's dog, I'd catch him for so much."

Neighbors sympathized as much as in them lay. It was the town talk; the meetings were held at Wolcott & Holden's. Every man told of his losses and disappointments in this line. One had heard of his pig last up in Westford, but never saw him again; another had only caught his pig by his running against a post so hard as to stun himself for a few moments. It was thought this one must have been born in the woods, for he would run and leap like a wolf. Some advised not to build so very high, but lay the upper board flat over the pen, for then, when he caught by his fore feet, his body would swing under to no purpose. One said you would not catch him to buy a pig out of a drove. Our pig ran as if he *still* had the devil in him. It was generally conceded that a good dog was the desideratum. But thereupon Lawrence, the harness-maker, came forward and told his experience. He once helped hunt a pig in the next town. He weighed two hundred; had been out some time (though not in '75), but they learned where he resorted; but they got a capital dog of the right kind. They had the dog tied lest he should scare the pig too soon. They crawled along very carefully near to the hollow where the pig was till they could hear him. They knew that if he should hear them and he was wide awake, he would dash off with a grunt, and that would be the last of him, but what more could they do? They consulted in a whisper and concluded to let the dog go. They did so, and directly heard an awful yelp; rushed up; the pig was gone, and there lay the dog torn all to pieces! At this there was a universal *haw! haw!* and the reputation of dogs fell, and the chance of catching the pig seemed less.

Two dollars reward was offered to him who would catch and return him without maiming him. At length, the 26th, he was heard from. He was caught and tied in north part of the town. Took to a swamp, as they say they are inclined. He was chased two hours with a spaniel dog, which never faced him, nor touched him, but, as the man said, "tuckered him out," kept him on the go and showed where he was. When at a distance the pig stopped and faced the dog until the pursuers came up. He was brought home the 27th, all his legs tied, and put into his new pen. It was a very deep one. It might have been made deeper, but Father did not wish to build a wall, and the man who caught him and got his two dollars for it thought it ought to hold any decent pig. Father said he didn't wish to keep him in a well.

Sept. 2. . . . There was an old gentleman here to-day who lived in Concord when he was young and remembers how Dr. Ripley talked to him and other little boys from the pulpit, as they came into church with their hands full of lilies, saying that those lilies looked so fresh that they must have been gathered that morning! Therefore they must have committed the sin of bathing this morning! Why, this is as sacred a river as the Ganges, sir. . . .

Oct. 18. . . . Men commonly exaggerate the theme. Some themes they think are significant and others insignificant. I feel that my life is very homely, my pleasures very cheap. Joy and sorrow, success and failure, grandeur and meanness, and indeed most words in the English language do not mean for me what they do for my neighbors. I see that my neighbors look with compassion on me, that they think it is a mean and unfortunate destiny which makes me to walk in these fields and woods so much and sail on this river alone. But so long as I find here the only real elysium, I cannot hesitate in my choice. My work is writing, and I do not hesitate, though I know that no subject is too trivial for me, tried by ordinary standards; for, ye fools, the theme is nothing, the life is everything. All that interests the reader is the depth and intensity of the life excited. We touch our subject but by a point which has no breadth, but the pyramid of our experience, or our interest in it, rests on us by a broader or narrower base. That is, man is all in all, Nature nothing, but as she draws him out and reflects him. Give me simple, cheap, and homely themes. . . .

1857

Jan. 7. . . . There is nothing so sanative, so poetic, as a walk in the woods and fields even now, when I meet none abroad for pleasure. Nothing so inspires me and excites such serene and profitable thought. The objects are elevating. In the street and in society I am almost invariably cheap and dissipated, my life is unspeakably mean. No amount of gold or respectability would in the least redeem it,—dining with the Governor or a member of Congress!! But alone in distant woods or fields, in unpretending sprout-lands or pastures tracked by rabbits, even in a bleak and, to most, cheerless day, like this, when a villager would be thinking of his inn, I come to myself, I once more feel myself grandly related, and that cold and solitude are friends of mine. I suppose that this value, in my case, is equivalent to what others get by churchgoing and prayer. I come to my solitary woodland walk as the homesick go home. I thus dispose of the superfluous and see things as they are, grand and beautiful. I have told many that I walk every day about half the daylight, but I think they do not believe it. I wish to get the Concord, the Massachusetts, the America, out of my head and be sane a part of every day. If there are missionaries for the heathen, why not send them to me? I wish to know something; I wish to be made better. I wish to forget, a considerable part of every day, all mean, narrow, trivial men (and this requires usually to forego and forget all personal relations so long), and therefore I come out to these solitudes, where the problem of existence is simplified. I get away a mile or two from the town into the stillness and solitude of nature, with rocks, trees, weeds, snow about me. I enter some glade in the woods, perchance, where a few weeds and dry leaves alone lift themselves above the surface of the snow, and it is as if I had come to an open window. I see out and around myself. Our *skylights* are thus far away from the ordinary resorts of men. I am not satisfied with ordinary windows. I must have a true *skylight*. My true skylight is on the outside of the village. I am not thus expanded, recreated, enlightened, when I meet a company of men. It chances that the sociable, the town and county, or the farmers' club does not prove a skylight to me. I do not invariably find myself translated under those circumstances. They bore me. The man I meet with is not often so instructive as the silence he breaks. This stillness, solitude, wildness of nature is a kind of thoroughwort, or boneset, to my intellect. This is what I go out to seek. It is as if I always met in those places some grand, serene, immortal, infinitely encouraging, though invisible, companion, and walked with him. There at last my nerves are steadied, my senses and my mind do their office. I am aware that most of my neighbors would think it a hardship to be compelled to linger here one hour, especially this bleak day, and yet I receive this sweet and ineffable compensation for it. It is the most agreeable thing I do. Truly, my coins are uncurrent with them. . . .

June 14. Sunday. 7 A. M. — To Clark's Island.

B. M. Watson tells me that he learns from pretty good authority that Webster once saw the sea-serpent. It seems it was first seen, in the bay between Manomet and Plymouth Beach, by a perfectly reliable witness (many years ago), who was accustomed to look out on the sea with his glass every morning the first thing as regularly as he ate his breakfast. One morning he saw this monster, with a head somewhat like a horse's raised some six feet above the water, and his body the size of a cask trailing behind. He was careering over the bay, chasing the mackerel, which ran ashore in their fright and were washed up and died in great numbers. The story is that Webster had appointed to meet some Plymouth gentlemen at Manomet and spend the day fishing with them. After the fishing was [over], he set out to return to Duxbury in his sailboat with Peterson, as he had come, and on the way they saw the sea-serpent, which answered to the common account of this creature. It passed directly across their bows only six or seven rods off and then disappeared. On the sail homeward, Webster having had time to reflect on what had occurred, at length said to Peterson, "For God's sake, never say a word about this to any one, for if it should be known that I have seen the sea-serpent, I should never hear the last of it, but wherever I went should have to tell the story to every one I met." So it has not leaked out till now.

Oct. 7. P. M. — To Cliffs and Walden.

Little chincapin oaks are partly turned, dull scarlet or yellow as it may happen, nearly in prime, not fallen. Some of their leaves (as well as of the white oak) are gnawed into lace regularly about the edges. Hornbeam generally green still, but becoming yellowish-brown and falling. Black alder, still green. Elder is greenish-yellow. I see *some* panicled andromeda dark-red or crimson. Swamp-pink a *dark* reddish purple where exposed. Beach plum begins to turn a clear pale yellow in dry places. Sage willow is fairly yellowing and some even falling.

Crossing Depot Brook, I see many yellow butterflies fluttering about the *Aster puniceus*, still abundantly in bloom there.

I go across Bartonia Meadow direct to Bear Garden Hill-side. Approaching the sand-slide, I see, some fifty rods off, looking toward the sun, the top of the maple swamp just appearing over the sheeny russet edge of the hill, — a strip, apparently twenty rods long and ten feet deep, of the most intensely brilliant scarlet, orange, and yellow, equal to any flowers or fruits or any tints ever painted. As I advance, lowering the edge of the hill, which makes the firm foreground or lower frame to the picture, the depth of this brilliant grove revealed steadily increases, suggesting that the whole of the concealed valley is filled with such color. As usual, there is one tree-top of an especially brilliant scarlet, with which the others contrast.

One wonders that the tithing-men and fathers of the town are not out to see what the trees mean by their high colors and exuberance of spirits, fearing that some mischief is brewing. I do not see what the Puritans did at that season when the maples blazed out in scarlet. They certainly could not have worshipped in groves then. Perhaps that is what they built meeting-houses and surrounded them with horse-sheds for.

No wonder we must have our annual cattle-show and fall training and perhaps Cornwallis, our September courts, etc. Nature holds her annual fair and gala-days in October in every hollow and on every hill-side.

Look into that hollow all aglow, where the trees are clothed in their vestures of most dazzling tints. Does it not suggest a thousand gypsies beneath, rows of booths, and that man's spirits should rise as high, that the routine of his life should be interrupted by an analogous festivity and rejoicing?

It is the reign of crickets now. You see them gliding busily about over all sunny surfaces. They sometimes get into my shoes; but oftener I have to empty out the seeds of various shrubs and weeds which I have been compelled to transport.

Looking toward the sun from Lupine Bank, I see bloody patches of blackberry vines amid the fine hoary and sheeny grass of the pasture. Since the frosts such pastures are already a hoary russet.

Some shrub oaks are yellow, others reddish.

When I turn round half-way up Fair Haven Hill, by the orchard wall, and look northwest, I am surprised for the thousandth time at the beauty of the landscape, and I sit down to behold it at my leisure. I think that Concord affords no better view. It is always incredibly fair, but ordinarily we are mere objects in it, and not witnesses of it. I see, through the bright

October air, a valley extending southwest and northeast and some two miles across, — so far I can see distinctly, — with a broad, yellow meadow tinged with brown at the bottom, and a blue river winding slowly through it northward, with a regular edging of low bushes on the brink, of the same color with the meadow. Skirting the meadow are straggling lines, and occasionally large masses a quarter of a mile wide, of brilliant scarlet and yellow and crimson trees, backed by and mingled with green forests and green and hoary russet fields and hills; and on the hills around shoot up a million scarlet and orange and yellow and crimson fires amid the green; and here and there amid the trees, often beneath the largest and most graceful of those which have brown-yellow dome-like tops, are bright white or gray houses; and beyond stretches a forest, wreath upon wreath, and between each two wreaths I know lies a similar vale; and far beyond all, on the verge of the horizon, are half a dozen dark-blue mountain-summits. Large birds of a brilliant blue and white plumage are darting and screaming amid the glowing foliage a quarter of a mile below, while smaller blue birds warble faintly but sweetly around me.

Such is the dwelling-place of man; but go to a caucus in the village to-night or to a church to-morrow, and see if there is anything said to suggest that the inhabitants of those houses know what kind of world they live in. But hark! I hear the tolling of a distant funeral bell, and they are conveying a corpse to the churchyard from one of the houses that I see, and its serious sound is more in harmony with this scenery than any ordinary bustle could be. It suggests that a man must die to his present life before he can appreciate his opportunities and the beauty of the abode that is appointed him.

I do not know how to entertain one who can't take long walks. The first thing that suggests itself is to get a horse to draw them, and that brings us at once into contact with stablers and dirty harness, and I do not get over my ride for a long time. I give up my forenoon to them and get along pretty well, the very elasticity of the air and promise of the day abetting me, but they are as heavy as dumplings by mid-afternoon. If they can't walk, why won't they take an honest nap and let me go in the afternoon? But, come two o'clock, they alarm me by an evident disposition to sit. In the midst of the most glorious Indian-summer afternoon, there they sit, breaking your chairs and wearing out the house, with their backs to the light, taking no note of the lapse of time.

As I sat on the high bank at the east end of Walden this afternoon, at five o'clock, I saw, by a peculiar intention or dividing of the eye, a very striking subaqueous rainbow-like phenomenon. A passer-by might, per-haps would, have noticed that the bright-tinted shrubs about the high shore on the sunny side were reflected from the water; but, unless on the alert for such effects, he would have failed to perceive the full beauty of the phenomenon. Unless you look for reflections, you commonly will not find them. Those brilliant shrubs, which were from three to a dozen feet in height, were all reflected, dimly so far as the details of leaves, etc., were concerned, but brightly as to color, and, of course, in the order in which they stood, — scarlet, yellow, green, etc.; but, there being a slight ripple on the surface, these reflections were not true to their height though true to their breadth, but were extended downward with mathematical perpendicularity, three or four times too far, forming sharp pyramids of the several colors, gradually reduced to mere dusky points. The effect of this prolongation of the reflection was a very pleasing softening and blending of the colors, especially when a small bush of one bright tint stood directly before another of a contrary and equally bright tint. It was just as if you were to brush firmly aside with your hand or a brush a fresh line of paint of various colors, or so many lumps of friable colored powders. There was, accordingly, a sort of belt, as wide as the whole height of the hill, extending downward along the whole north or sunny side of the pond, composed of exceedingly short and narrow inverted pyramids of the most brilliant colors intermixed. I have seen, indeed, similar inverted pyramids in the old drawings of tattooing about the waists of the aborigines of this country. Walden, too, like an Indian maiden, wears this broad rainbow-like belt of brilliant-colored points or cones round her waist in October. The color seems to be reflected and re-reflected from ripple to ripple, losing brightness each time by the softest possible gradation, and tapering toward the beholder, since he occupies a mere point of view. This is one of the prettiest effects of the autumnal change.

The harvest of leaves is at hand in some valleys, and generally the young deciduous trees on hillsides have the brilliant tint of ripe fruits. Already many windfalls strew the ground under the maples and elms, etc. I see one or two maple shrubs quite bare, while many large maples are still quite green.

In that rainbow belt we have color, which is commonly so rare and precious and confined to precious stones, in the utmost profusion. The ripples convey the reflection toward us, till all the color is winnowed out and spilled between them and only the dusky points reach near to this side where we stand. It is as if a broad belt (or waist-cloth) of sharp and narrow inverted cones or pyramids of bright colors, softly blended like fairy worsted work, their bases rising to a line mathematically level about the waist of the pond. That fall river Indian, like the Almouchicois generally, wore a belt of hollow tubes.

It was strange that only the funeral bell was in harmony with that scene, while other sounds were too frivolous and trivial, as if only through the gate of death would man come to appreciate his opportunities and the beauty of the world he has abused. In proportion as death is more earnest than life, it is better than life. . . .

Nov. 29. . . . A week or so ago, as I learn, Miss Emeline Barnett told a little boy who boards with her, and who was playing with an open knife in his hand, that he must be careful not to fall down and cut himself with it, for once Mr. David Loring, when he was a little boy, fell down with a knife in his hand and cut his throat badly. It was soon reported, among the children at least, that little David Loring, the grandson of the former, had fallen down with a knife in his hand as he was going to school, and nearly cut his throat; next, that Mr. David Loring the grandfather (who lives in Framingham) had committed suicide, had cut his throat, was not dead, indeed, but was not expected to live; and in this form the story spread like wildfire over the town and county. Nobody expressed surprise. His oldest acquaintances and best friends, his legal adviser, all said, "Well, I can believe it." He was known by many to have been speculating in Western lands, which, owing to the hard times, was a failure, and he was depressed in consequence. Sally Cummings helped spread the news. Said there was no doubt of it, but there was Fay's wife (L.'s daughter) knew nothing of it yet, they were as merry as crickets over there. Others stated that Wetherbee, the expressman, had been over to Northboro, and learned that Mr. Loring had taken poison in Northboro. Mr. Rhodes was stated to have received a letter from Mr. Robbins of Framingham giving all the particulars. Mr. Wild, it was said, had also got a letter from his son Silas in Framingham, to whom he had written, which confirmed the report. As Wild went down-town, he met Meeks the carpenter and inquired in a significant way if he got anything new. Meeks simply answered, "Well, David Loring won't eat another Thanksgiving dinner." A child at school wrote to her parents at Northboro, telling the news. Mrs. Loring's sister lives there, and it chances that her husband committed suicide. They were, therefore, slow to communicate the news to her, but at length could not contain themselves longer and told it. The sister was terribly affected; wrote to her son (L.'s nephew) in Worcester, who immediately took the cars and went to Framingham and when he arrived there met his uncle just putting his family into the cars. He shook his hand very heartily indeed, looking, however, hard at his throat, but said not a word about his errand. Already doubts had arisen, people were careful how they spoke of it, the expressmen were mum, Adams and Wetherbee never said Loring. The Framingham expressman used the same room with Adams in Boston. A. simply asked, "Any news from Framingham this morning? Seen Loring lately?" and learned that all was well.

1858

April 30. . . . I learn that one farmer, seeing me standing a long time still in the midst of a pool (I was watching for hylodes), said that it was his father, who had been drinking some of Pat Haggerty's rum, and had lost his way home. So, setting out to lead him home, he discovered that it was I. . . .

June 7. . . . As I was wading in this Wyman meadow, looking for bullfrog-spawn, I saw a hole at the bottom, where it was six or eight inches deep, by the side of a mass of mud and weeds which rose just to the surface three or four feet from the shore. It was about five inches in diameter, with some sand at the mouth, just like a musquash's hole. As I stood there within two feet, a pout put her head out, as if to see who was there, and directly came forth and disappeared under the target-weed; but as I stood perfectly still, waiting for the water which I had disturbed to settle about the hole, she circled round and round several times between me and the hole, cautiously, stealthily approaching the entrance but as often withdrawing, and at last mustered courage to enter it. I then noticed another similar hole in the same mass, two or three feet from this. I thrust my arm into the first, running it in and downward about fifteen inches. It was a little more than a foot long and enlarged somewhat at the end, the bottom, also, being about a foot beneath the surface, — for it slanted downward, — but I felt nothing within; I only felt a pretty regular and rounded apartment with firm walls of weedy or fibrous mud. I then thrust my arm into the other hole, which was longer and deeper, but at first discovered nothing; but, trying again, I found that I had not reached the end, for it turned a little and descended more than I supposed. Here I felt a similar apartment or enlargement, some six inches in diameter horizontally but not quite so high nor nearly so wide at its throat. Here, to my surprise, I felt something soft, like a gelatinous mass of spawn, but, feeling a little further, felt the horns of a pout. I deliberately took hold of her by the head and lifted her out of the hole and the water, having run my arm in two thirds its length. She offered not the slightest resistance from first to last, even when I held her out of water before my face, and only darted away suddenly when I dropped her in the water. The entrance to her apartment was so narrow that she could hardly have escaped if I had tried to prevent her. Putting in my arm again, I felt, under where she had been, a flattish mass of ova, several inches in diameter, resting on the mud, and took out some. Feeling again in the first hole, I found as much more there. Though I had been stepping round and over the second nest for several minutes, I had not scared the pout. The ova of the first nest already contained white wiggling young. I saw no motion in the others. The ova in each case were dull-yellowish and the size of small buckshot. These nests did not communicate with each other and had no other outlet.

Pouts, then, make their nests in shallow mud-holes or bays, in masses of weedy mud, or probably in the muddy bank; and the old pout hovers over the spawn or keeps guard at the entrance. Where do the Walden pouts breed when they have not access to this meadow? The first pout, whose eggs were most developed, was the largest and had some slight wounds on the back. The other may have been the male in the act of fertilizing the ova. . . .

Nov. 4. . . . Nature does not cast pearls before swine. There is just as much beauty visible to us in the landscape as we are prepared to appreciate, — not a grain more. The actual objects which one person will see from a particular hilltop are just as different from those which another will see as the persons are different. The scarlet oak must, in a sense, be in your eye when you go forth. We cannot see anything until we are possessed with the idea of it, and then we can hardly see anything else. In my botanical rambles I find that first the idea, or image, of a plant occupies my thoughts, though it may at first seem very foreign to this locality, and for some weeks or months I go thinking of it and expecting it unconsciously, and at length I surely see it, and it is henceforth an actual neighbor of mine. This is the history of my finding a score or more of rare plants which I could name. . . .

Nov. 9. . . . Now the young hen-hawks, full-grown but inexperienced, still white-breasted and brown (not red)-tailed, swoop down after the farmer's hens, between the barn and the house, often carrying one off in their clutches, and all the rest of the pack half fly, half run, to the barn. Unwarrantably bold, one ventures to stoop before the farmer's eyes. He clutches in haste his trusty gun, which hangs, ready loaded, on its pegs; he pursues warily to where the marauder sits teetering on a lofty pine, and when he is sailing scornfully away he meets his fate and comes fluttering head forward to earth. The exulting farmer hastes to secure his trophy. He treats the proud bird's body with indignity. He carries it home to show his wife and children, for the hens were his wife's special care. He thinks it one of his best shots, full thirteen rods. This gun is "an *all-fired* good piece" — nothing but robin-shot. The body of the victim is delivered up to the children and the dog and, like the body of Hector, is dragged so many times round Troy.

But alas for the youthful hawk, the proud bird of prey, the tenant of the skies! We shall no more see his wave-like outline against a cloud, nor hear his scream from behind one. He saw but a pheasant in the field, the food which nature has provided for him, and stooped to seize it. This was his offense. He, the native of these skies, must make way for those bog-trotters from another land, which never soar. The eye that was conversant with sublimity, that looked down on earth from under its sharp projecting brow, is closed; the head that was never made dizzy by any height is brought low; the feet that were not made to walk on earth now lie useless along it. With those trailing claws for grapnels it dragged the lower sky. Those wings which swept the sky must now dust the chimney-corner, perchance. So weaponed, with strong beak and talons, and wings, like a war-steamer, to carry them about. In vain were the brown-spotted eggs laid, in vain were ye cradled in the loftiest pine of the swamp. Where are your father and mother? Will they hear of your early death? before ye had acquired your full plumage, they who nursed and defended ye so faithfully?

Nov. 16. . . . Preaching? Lecturing? Who are ye that ask for these things? What do ye want to hear, ye puling infants? A trumpet-sound that would train you up to mankind, or a nurse's lullaby? The preachers and lecturers deal with men of straw, as they are men of straw themselves. Why, a free-spoken man, of sound lungs, cannot draw a long breath without causing your rotten institutions to come toppling down by the vacuum he makes. Your church is a baby-house made of blocks, and so of the state. It would be a relief to breathe one's self occasionally among men. If there were any magnanimity in us, any grandeur of soul, anything but sects and parties undertaking to patronize God and keep the mind within bounds, how often we might encourage and provoke one another by a free expression! I will not consent to walk with my mouth muzzled, not till I am rabid, until there is danger that I shall bite the unoffending and that my bite will produce hydrophobia.

Freedom of speech! It hath not entered into your hearts to conceive what those words mean. It is not leave given me by your sect to say this or that; it is when leave is given to your sect to withdraw. The church, the state, the school, the magazine, think they are liberal and free! It is the freedom of a prison-yard. I ask only that one fourth part of my honest thoughts be spoken aloud. What is it you tolerate, you church to-day? Not truth, but a lifelong hypocrisy. Let us have institutions framed not out of our rottenness, but out of our soundness. This factitious piety is like stale gingerbread. I would like to suggest what a pack of fools and cowards we mankind are. They want me to agree not to breathe too hard in the neighborhood of their paper castles. If I should draw a long breath in the neighborhood of these institutions, their weak and flabby sides would fall out, for my own inspiration would exhaust the air about them. The church! it is eminently the timid institution, and the heads and pillars of it are constitutionally and by principle the greatest cowards in the community. The voice that goes up from the monthly concerts is not so brave and so cheering as that which rises from the frog-ponds of the land. The best "preachers," so called, are an effeminate class; their bravest thoughts wear petticoats. If they have any manhood they are sure to forsake the ministry, though they were to turn their attention to baseball. Look at your editors of popular magazines. I have dealt with two or three the most liberal of them. They are afraid to print a whole sentence, a *round* sentence, a free-spoken sentence. They want to get thirty thousand subscribers, and they will do anything to get them. They consult the D.D.'s and all the letters of the alphabet before printing a sentence. I have been into many of these cowardly New England towns where they *profess* Christianity, — invited to speak, perchance, — where they were trembling in their shoes at the thought of the things you might say, as if they knew their weak side, — that they were weak on all sides. The devil they have covenanted with is a timid devil. If they would let their sores alone they might heal, and they could to the wars again like men; but instead of that they get together in meeting-house cellars, rip off the bandages and poultice them with sermons.

One of our New England towns is sealed up hermetically like a molasses-hogshead, — such is its sweet Christianity, — only a little of the sweet trickling out at the cracks enough to daub you. The few more liberal-minded or indifferent inhabitants are the flies that buzz about it. It is Christianity bunged up. I see awful eyes looking out through a bull's-eye at the bung-hole. It is doubtful if they can fellowship with me.

The further you go up country, I think the worse it is, the more benighted they are. On the one side you will find a barroom which holds the "Scoffers," so called, on the other a vestry where is a monthly concert of prayer. There is just as little to cheer you in one of these companies as the other. It may be often the truth and righteousness of the barroom that saves the town. There is nothing to redeem the bigotry and moral cowardice of New-Englanders in my eyes. You may find a cape which runs six miles into the sea that has not a man of moral courage upon it. What is called faith is an immense prejudice. Like the Hindoos and Russians [?] and Sandwich-Islanders (that were), they are the creatures of an institution. They do not think; they adhere like oysters to what their fathers and grandfathers adhered to. How often is it that the shoemaker, by thinking over his last, can think as valuable a thought as he makes a valuable shoe?

I have been into the town, being invited to speak to the inhabitants, not valuing, not having read even, the Assembly's Catechism, and I try to stimulate them by reporting the best of my experience. I see the craven priest looking round for a hole to escape at, alarmed because it was he that invited me thither, and an awful silence pervades the audience. They think they will never get me there again. But the seed has not all fallen in stony and shallow ground. . . .

1859

March 11. . . . E. Hosmer says that a man told him that he had seen my uncle Charles take a twelve-foot ladder, set it up straight, and then run up and down the other side, kicking it from behind him as he went down. E. H. told of seeing him often at the tavern toss his hat to the ceiling, twirling it over, and catch it on his head every time. . . .

May 2. . . . I feel no desire to go to California or Pike's Peak, but I often think at night with inexpressible satisfaction and yearning of the *arrowheadiferous* sands of Concord. I have often spent whole afternoons, especially in the spring, pacing back and forth over a sandy field, looking for these relics of a race. This is the gold which our sands yield. The soil of that rocky spot on Simon Brown's land is quite ash-colored — now that the sod is turned up — by Indian fires, with numerous pieces of coal in it. There is a great deal of this ash-colored soil in the country. We do literally plow up the hearths of a people and plant in their ashes. The ashes of their fires color much of our soil.

Oct. 15. . . . Each town should have a park, or rather a primitive forest, of five hundred or a thousand acres, where a stick should never be cut for fuel, a common possession forever, for instruction and recreation. We hear of cow-commons and ministerial lots, but we want *men*-commons and lay lots, inalienable forever. Let us keep the New World *new*, preserve all the advantages of living in the country. There is meadow and pasture and wood-lot for the town's poor. Why not a forest and huckleberry-field for the town's rich? All Walden Wood might have been preserved for our park forever, with Walden in its midst, and the Easterbrooks Country, an unoccupied area of some four square miles, might have been our huckleberry-field. If any owners of these tracts are about to leave the world without natural heirs who need or deserve to be specially remembered, they will do wisely to abandon their possession to all, and not will them to some individual who perhaps has enough already. As some give to Harvard College or another institution, why might not another give a forest or huckleberry-field to Concord? A town is an institution which deserves to be remembered. We boast of our system of education, but why stop at schoolmasters and schoolhouses? We are all schoolmasters, and our schoolhouse is the universe. To attend chiefly to the desk or schoolhouse while we neglect the scenery in which it is placed is absurd. If we do not look out we shall find our fine schoolhouse standing in a cow-yard at last. . . .

1860

June 10. . . . There is much handsome interrupted fern in the Painted-Cup Meadow, and near the top of one of the clumps we noticed something like a large cocoon, the color of the rusty cinnamon fern wool. It was a red bat, the New York bat, so called. It hung suspended, head directly downward, with its little sharp claws or hooks caught through one of the divisions at the base of one of the pinnæ, above the fructification. It was a delicate rusty brown in color, very like the wool of the cinnamon fern, with the whiter bare spaces seen through it early in the season. I thought at first glance it was a broad brown cocoon, then that it was the plump body of a monstrous emperor moth. It was rusty or reddish brown, white or hoary within or beneath the tips, with a white apparently triangular spot beneath, about the insertion of the wings. Its wings were very compactly folded up, the principal bones (darker-reddish) lying flat along the under side of its body, and a hook on each meeting its opposite under the chin of the creature. It did not look like fur, but more like the plush of the ripe cat-tail head, though more loose, — all trembling in the wind and with the pulsations of the animal. I broke off the top of the fern and let the bat lie on its back in my hand. I held it and turned it about for ten or fifteen minutes, but it did not awake. Once or twice it opened its eyes a little, and even it raised its head, opened its mouth, but soon drowsily dropped its head and fell asleep again. Its ears were rounded and nearly bare. It was more attentive to sounds than to motions. Finally, by shaking it, and especially by hissing or whistling, I thoroughly awakened it, and it fluttered off twenty or thirty rods to the woods. I cannot but think that its instinct taught it to cling to the interrupted fern, since it might readily be mistaken for a mass of its fruit. Raised its old-haggish head. Unless it showed its head wide awake, it looked like a tender infant.

Aug. 1. P. M. — To Cliffs.
The earliest corn has shed its pollen, say a week or ten days. Rye, wheat, and oats and barley have bloomed, say a month.

I stand at the wall-end on the Cliffs and look over the Miles meadow on Conantum. It is an unusually clear day after yesterday's rain.

How much of beauty — of color, as well as form — on which our eyes daily rest goes unperceived by us! No one but a botanist is likely to distinguish nicely the different shades of green with which the open surface of the earth is clothed, — not even a landscape-painter if he does not know the species of sedges and grasses which paint it. With respect to the color of grass, most of those even who attend peculiarly to the aspects of Nature only observe that it is more or less dark or light, green or brown, or velvety, fresh or parched, etc. But if you are studying grasses you look for another and different beauty, and you find it, in the wonderful variety of color, etc., presented by the various species. Take the bare, unwooded earth now, and consider the beautiful variety of shades (or tints?) of green that clothe it under a bright sun. The pastured hills of Conantum, now just imbrowned (probably by the few now stale flowering tops of the red-top which the cows have avoided as too wiry), present a hard and solid green or greenish brown, just touched here and there delicately with light patches of sheep's fescue (though it may be only its radical leaves left), as if a dew lay on it there, — and this has some of the effect of a watered surface, — and the whole is dotted with a thousand little shades of projecting rocks and shrubs. Then, looking lower at the meadow in Miles's field, that is seen as a bright-yellow and sunny stream (yet with a slight tinge of glaucous) between the dark-green potato-fields, flowing onward with windings and expansions, and, as it were, with rips and waterfalls, to the river meadows.

Again, I sit on the brow of the orchard, and look northwest down the river valley (at mid-afternoon). There flows, or rests, the calm blue winding river, lake-like, with its smooth silver-plated sides, and wherever weeds extend across it, there too the silver plate bridges it, like a spirit's bridge across the Styx; but the rippled portions are blue as the sky. This river reposes in the midst of a broad brilliant yellow valley amid green fields and hills and woods, as if, like the Nanking or Yang-ho (or what-not), it flowed through an Oriental Chinese meadow where yellow is the imperial color. The immediate and raised edge of the river, with its willows and button-bushes and polygonums, is a light green, but the immediately adjacent low meadows, where the sedge prevails, is a brilliant and cheerful yellow, intensely, incredibly bright, such color as you never see in pictures; yellow of various tints, in the lowest and sedgiest parts deepening to so much color as if gamboge had been rubbed into the meadow there; the most cheering color in all the landscape; shaded with little darker isles of green in the midst of this yellow sea of sedge. Yet it is the bright and cheerful yellow, as of spring, and with nothing in the least autumnal in it. How this contrasts with the adjacent fields of red-top, now fast falling before the scythe!

When your attention has been drawn to them, nothing is more charming than the common colors of the earth's surface. See yonder flashing field of corn through the *shimmering* air. (This was said day before yesterday.)

The deciduous woods generally have now and for a long time been nearly as dark as the pines, though, unlike the pines, they show a general silveriness. . . .

Aug. 22. . . . The recent heavy rains have washed away the bank here considerably, and it looks and smells more mouldy with human relics than ever. I therefore find myself inevitably exploring it. On the edge of the ravine whose beginning I witnessed, one foot beneath the surface and just over a layer some three inches thick of pure shells and ashes, — a gray-white line on the face of the cliff. — I find several pieces of Indian pottery with a rude ornament on it, not much more red than the earth itself. Looking farther, I find more fragments, which have been washed down the sandy slope in a stream, as far as ten feet. I find in all thirty-one pieces, averaging an inch in diameter and about a third of an inch thick. Several of them made part of the upper edge of the vessel, and other line on the narrow edge itself. At first I thought to match the pieces again, like a geographical puzzle, but I did not find that any I [got] belonged together. The vessel must have been quite large, and I have not got nearly all of it. It appears to have been an impure clay with much sand and gravel in it, and I think a little pounded shell. It is [of] very unequal thickness, some of the unadorned pieces (probably the bottom) being half an inch thick, while near the edge it is not more than a quarter of an inch thick. There was under this spot and under the layer of shells a manifest hollowness in the ground, not yet filled up. I find many small pieces of bone in the soil of this bank, probably of animals the Indians ate.

In another part of the bank, in the midst of a much larger heap of shells which has been exposed, I found a delicate stone tool of this form and size: of a soft slate-stone. It is very thin and sharp on each side edge, and in the middle is not more than an eighth of an inch thick. I suspect that this was used to open clams with.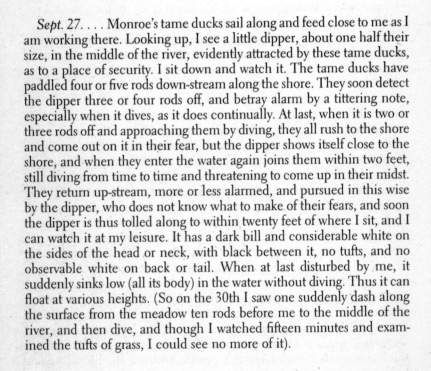

It is curious that I had expected to find as much as this, and in this very spot too, before I reached it (I mean the pot). Indeed, I never find a remarkable Indian relic — and I find a good many — but I have first divined its existence, and planned the discovery of it. Frequently I have told myself distinctly what it was to be before I found it. . . .

Sept. 27. . . . Monroe's tame ducks sail along and feed close to me as I am working there. Looking up, I see a little dipper, about one half their size, in the middle of the river, evidently attracted by these tame ducks, as to a place of security. I sit down and watch it. The tame ducks have paddled four or five rods down-stream along the shore. They soon detect the dipper three or four rods off, and betray alarm by a tittering note, especially when it dives, as it does continually. At last, when it is two or three rods off and approaching them by diving, they all rush to the shore and come out on it in their fear, but the dipper shows itself close to the shore, and when they enter the water again joins them within two feet, still diving from time to time and threatening to come up in their midst. They return up-stream, more or less alarmed, and pursued in this wise by the dipper, who does not know what to make of their fears, and soon the dipper is thus tolled along to within twenty feet of where I sit, and I can watch it at my leisure. It has a dark bill and considerable white on the sides of the head or neck, with black between it, no tufts, and no observable white on back or tail. When at last disturbed by me, it suddenly sinks low (all its body) in the water without diving. Thus it can float at various heights. (So on the 30th I saw one suddenly dash along the surface from the meadow ten rods before me to the middle of the river, and then dive, and though I watched fifteen minutes and examined the tufts of grass, I could see no more of it).

Oct. 10. . . . P. M. — Went to a fire — or smoke — at Mrs. Hoar's. There is a slight blaze and more smoke. Two or three hundred men rush to the house, cut large holes in the roof, throw many hogsheads of water into it, — when a few pails full well directed would suffice, — and then they run off again, leaving your attic three inches deep with water, which is rapidly descending through the ceiling to the basement and spoiling all that can be spoiled, while a torrent is running down the stairways. They were very forward to put out the [fire], but they take no pains to put out the water, which does far more damage. The first was amusement; the last would be mere work and utility. Why is there not a little machine invented to throw the water out of a house?

They are hopelessly cockneys everywhere who learn to swim with a machine. They take neither disease nor health, nay, nor life itself, the natural way. I see dumb-bells in the minister's study, and some of their dumbness gets into his sermons. Some travellers carry them round the world in their carpetbags. Can he be said to travel who requires still this exercise? A party of school-children had a picnic at the Easterbrooks Country the other [day], and they carried bags of beans from their gymnasium to exercise with there. I cannot be interested in these extremely artificial amusements. The traveller is no longer a wayfarer, with his staff and pack and dusty coat. He is not a pilgrim, but he travels in a saloon, and carries dumb-bells to exercise with in the intervals of his journey.

Nov. 9. 12 M. — To Inches' Woods in Boxboro.

This wood is some one and three quarters miles from West Acton, whither we went by railroad. It is in the east part of Boxboro, on both sides of the Harvard turnpike. We walked mostly across lots from West Acton to a part of the wood about half a mile north of the turnpike, — and the woods appeared to reach as much further north. We then walked in the midst of the wood in a southwesterly by west direction, about three quarters of a mile, crossing the turnpike west of the maple swamp and the brook, and thence south by east nearly as much more, — all the way in the woods, and chiefly old oak wood. The old oak wood, as we saw from the bare hill at the south end, extends a great deal further west and northwest, as well as north, than we went, and must be at least a mile and a half from north to south by a mile to a mile and a quarter *possibly* from east to west. Or there *may* be a thousand acres of old oak wood. The large wood is chiefly oak, and that white oak, though black, red, and scarlet oak are also common. White pine is in considerable quantity, and large pitch pine is scattered here and there, and saw some chestnut at the south end. Saw no hemlock or birch to speak of.

Beginning at the north end of our walk, the trees which I measured were (all at three feet from ground except when otherwise stated): a black oak, ten feet [in] circumference, trunk tall and of regular form; scarlet oak, seven feet three inches, by Guggins Brook; white oak, eight feet; white oak, ten feet, forks at ten feet; white oak, fifteen feet (at two and a half feet, bulging very much near ground; trunk of a pyramidal form; first branch at sixteen feet; this just north of turnpike and near Guggins Brook); white oak, nine feet four inches (divides to two at five feet); white oak, nine feet six inches (divides to two at five feet); red oak, eight feet (south of road); white pine, nine feet; a scarlet or red oak stump cut, twenty and a half inches [in] diameter, one hundred and sixty rings.

I was pleased to find that the largest of the white oaks, growing thus in a dense wood, often with a pine or other tree within two or three feet, were of pasture oak size and even form, the largest commonly branching low. Very many divide to two trunks at four or five feet only from the ground. You see some white oaks and even some others in the midst of the wood nearly as spreading as in open land.

Looking from the high bare hill at the south end, the limits of the *old* oak wood (so far as we could overlook it) were very distinct, its tops being a mass of gray brush, — contorted and intertwisted twigs and boughs, — while the younger oak wood around it, or bounding it, though still of respectable size, was still densely clothed with the reddish-brown leaves.

This famous oak lot — like Blood's and Wetherbee's — is a place of resort for those who hunt the gray squirrel. They have their leafy nests in the oak-tops.

It is an endless maze of gray oak trunks and boughs stretching far around. The great mass of individual trunks which you stand near is very impressive.

Many sturdy trunks (they commonly stand a little aslant) are remarkably straight and round, and have so much regularity in their roughness as to suggest smoothness. The older or largest white oaks were of a rougher and darker bark than Wetherbee's and Blood's, though often betraying the same tendency to smoothness, as if a rough layer had been stripped off near the ground.

I noticed that a great many trunks (the bark) had been gnawed near the ground, — different kinds of oak and chestnut, — perhaps by squirrels.

Nov. 10. Cheney gives me a little history of the Inches Woods. He says it was a grant to Jekil (John (?) Jekil) by the crown, and that it amounted to half of Boxboro as well as much of Stow and Acton. That Jekil had a summer house where Squire Hosmer's house stands in Stow, before the Revolution, but at that time withdrew into Boston. It was a great event when he used to come out to Stow in the summer. Boxboro was a part of Stow then. Mr. Hosmer had charge of the lands for Inches, and the kitchen of his house was partly the old summer house of Jekil, and he also remembered an old negro named York, who had been a slave of Jekil, and he, the negro, said that twenty of the thirty acres bought of Inches by Hosmer, behind his house, was once fenced in with a paling or picket fence ten or fifteen feet high, and formed a park in which Jekil kept deer. The neighbors used to come and peep through the paling at the deer. Henderson Inches, hearing of these lands about the time of the Revolution, went to the heirs of Jekil and purchased the whole tract quite cheap, and they had been a fortune to the family since. Many farms have been made of parts of the wood, and thousands of dollars' worth of wood have been sold at a time. Had realized maybe $150,000 from it. Cheney had heard that there were about four hundred acres of the Inches lands left. Henderson Inches died two or three years ago, and now his heirs wished to sell, but would not divide it, but sell in one body. Ruggles, Nourse, and Mason wished to buy, but not the whole. Except what has been sold, or generally, Inches would not have it cut. He was sharp and stood out for his price, and also liked to keep it. Hence it is a primitive oak wood and said to be the most of one in Massachusetts. . . .

1861

Jan. 30. . . . What are the natural features which make a township handsome? A river, with its waterfalls and meadows, a lake, a hill, a cliff or individual rocks, a forest, and ancient trees standing singly. Such things are beautiful; they have a high use which dollars and cents never represent. If the inhabitants of a town were wise, they would seek to preserve these things, though at a considerable expense; for such things educate far more than any hired teachers or preachers, or any at present recognized system of school education. I do not think him fit to be the founder of a state or even of a town who does not foresee the use of these things, but legislates chiefly for oxen, as it were.

Far the handsomest thing I saw in Boxboro was its noble oak wood. I doubt if there is a finer one in Massachusetts. Let her keep it a century longer, and men will make pilgrimages to it from all parts of the country; and yet it would be very like the rest of New England if Boxboro were ashamed of that woodland.

I have since heard, however, that she is contented to have that forest stand instead of the houses and farms that might supplant [it], because the land pays a much larger tax to the town now than it would then.

I said to myself, if the history of this town is written, the chief stress is probably laid on its parish and there is not a word about this forest in it.

It would be worth the while if in each town there were a committee appointed to see that the beauty of the town received no detriment. If we have the largest boulder in the county, then it should not belong to an individual, nor be made into door-steps.

As in many countries precious metals belong to the crown, so here more precious natural objects of rare beauty should belong to the public.

Not only the channel but one or both banks of every river should be a public highway. The only use of a river is not to float on it.

Think of a mountain-top in the township — even to the minds of the Indians a sacred place — only accessible through private grounds! a temple, as it were, which you cannot enter except by trespassing and at the risk of letting out or letting in somebody's cattle! in fact the temple itself in this case private property and standing in a man's cow-yard, — for such is commonly the case!

New Hampshire courts have lately been deciding — as if it was for them to decide — whether the top of Mt. Washington belonged to A or to B; and, it being decided in favor of B, as I hear, he went up one winter with the proper officer and took formal possession of it. But I think that the top of Mt. Washington should not be private property; it should be left unappropriated for modesty and reverence's sake, or if only to suggest that earth has higher uses than we put her to. I know it is a mere figure of speech to talk about temples nowadays, when men recognize none, and, indeed, associate the word with heathenism. . . .

Feb. 15. . . . A kitten is so flexible that she is almost double; the hind parts are equivalent to another kitten with which the fore part plays. She does not discover that her tail belongs to her till you tread upon it.

How eloquent she can be with her tail! Its sudden swellings and vibrations! She jumps into a chair and then stands on her hind legs to look out the window; looks steadily at objects far and near, first turning her gaze to this side then to that, for she loves to look out a window as much as any gossip. Ever and anon she bends back her ears to hear what is going on within the room, and all the while her eloquent tail is reporting the progress and success of her survey by speaking gestures which betray her interest in what she sees.

Then what a delicate hint she can give with her tail! passing perhaps underneath, as you sit at table, and letting the tip of her tail just touch your legs, as much as to say, I am here and ready for that milk or meat, though she may not be so forward as to look round at you when she emerges.

Only skin-deep lies the feral nature of the cat, unchanged still. I just had the misfortune to rock on to our cat's leg, as she was lying playfully spread out under my chair. Imagine the sound that arose, and which was excusable; but what will you say to the fierce growls and flashing eyes with which she met me for a quarter of an hour thereafter? No tiger in its jungle could have been savager.

May 14. . . . It is amusing to observe how a kitten regards the attic, kitchen, or shed where it was bred as its castle to resort to in time of danger. It loves best to sleep on some elevated place, as a shelf or chair, and for many months does not venture far from the back door where it first saw the light. Two rods is a great range for it, but so far it is tempted, when the dew is off, by the motions of grasshoppers and crickets and other such small game, sufficiently novel and surprising to it. They frequently have a wheezing cough, which some refer to grasshoppers' wings across their windpipes. The kitten has been eating grasshoppers.

If some member of the household with whom they are familiar — their mistress or master — goes forth into the garden, they are then encouraged to take a wider range, and for a short season explore the more distant bean and cabbage rows, or, if several of the family go forth at once, — as it were a reconnaissance in force, — the kitten does a transient scout duty outside, but yet on the slightest alarm they are seen bounding back with great leaps over the grass toward the castle, where they stand panting on the door-step, with their small lower jaws fallen, until they fill up with courage again. A cat looks down with complacency on the strange dog from the corn-barn window.

The kitten when it is two or three months old is full of play. Ever and anon she takes up her plaything in her mouth and carries it to another place, — a distant corner of the room or some other nook, as under a rocker, — or perchance drops it at your feet, seeming to delight in the mere carriage of it, as if it were her prey — tiger-like. In proportion to her animal spirits are her quick motions and sudden whirlings about on the carpet or in the air. She may make a great show of scratching and biting, but let her have your hand and she will presently lick it instead.

They are so naturally stealthy, skulking and creeping about, affecting holes and darkness, that they will enter a shed rather by some hole under the door-sill than go over the sill through the open door.

Though able to bear cold, few creatures love warmth more or sooner find out where the fire is. The cat, whether she comes home wet or dry, directly squeezes herself under the cooking-stove, and stews her brain there, if permitted. If the cat is in the kitchen, she is most likely to be found under the stove.

[Undated]. The kitten can already spit at a fortnight old, and it can mew from the first, though it often makes the motion of mewing without uttering any sound.

The cat about to bring forth seeks out some dark and secret place for the purpose, not frequented by other cats.

The kittens' ears are at first nearly concealed in the fur, and at a fortnight old they are mere broad-based triangles with a side foremost. But the old cat is ears for them at present, and comes running hastily to their aid when she hears them mew and licks them into contentment again. Even at three weeks the kitten cannot fairly walk, but only creeps feebly with outspread legs. But thenceforth its ears visibly though gradually lift and sharpen themselves.

At three weeks old the kitten begins to walk in a staggering and creeping manner and even to play a little with its mother, and, if you put your ear close, you may hear it purr. It is remarkable that it will not wander far from the dark corner where the cat has left it, but will instinctively find its way back to it, probably by the sense of touch, and will rest nowhere else. Also it is careful not to venture too near the edge of a precipice, and its claws are ever extended to save itself in such places. It washes itself somewhat, and assumes many of the attitudes of an old cat at this age. By the disproportionate size of its feet and head and legs now it reminds you [of] a lion.

I saw it scratch its ear to-day, probably for the first time; yet it lifted one of its hind legs and scratched its ear as effectually as an old cat does. So this is instinctive, and you may say that, when a kitten's ear first itches, Providence comes to the rescue and lifts its hind leg for it. You would say that this little creature was as perfectly protected by its instinct in its infancy as an old man can be by his wisdom. I observed when she first noticed the figures on the carpet, and also put up her paws to touch or play with surfaces a foot off. By the same instinct that they find the mother's teat before they can see they scratch their ears and guard against falling.

After a violent easterly storm in the night, which clears up at noon (November 3, 1861), I notice that the surface of the railroad causeway, composed of gravel, is singularly marked, as if stratified like some slate rocks, on their edges, so that I can tell within a small fraction of a degree from what quarter the rain came. These lines, as it were of stratification, are perfectly parallel, and straight as a ruler, diagonally across the flat surface of the causeway for its whole length. Behind each little pebble, as a protecting boulder, an eighth or a tenth of an inch in diameter, extends north-west a ridge of sand an inch or more, which it has protected from being washed away, while the heavy drops driven almost horizontally have washed out a furrow on each side, and on all sides are these ridges, half an inch apart and perfectly parallel.

All this is perfectly distinct to an observant eye, and yet could easily pass unnoticed by most. Thus each wind is self-registering.

END OF SELECTION

All books complete and unabridged. All 5³⁄₁₆″ × 8¼″, paperbound.
Just $1.00–$2.00 in U.S.A.

POETRY

GREAT LOVE POEMS, Shane Weller (ed.). 128pp. 27284-2 $1.00

SELECTED POEMS, Walt Whitman. 128pp. 26878-0 $1.00

THE BALLAD OF READING GAOL AND OTHER POEMS, Oscar Wilde. 64pp. 27072-6 $1.00

FAVORITE POEMS, William Wordsworth. 80pp. 27073-4 $1.00

EARLY POEMS, William Butler Yeats. 128pp. 27808-5 $1.00

FICTION

FLATLAND: A ROMANCE OF MANY DIMENSIONS, Edwin A. Abbott. 96pp. 27263-X $1.00

BEOWULF, Beowulf (trans. by R. K. Gordon). 64pp. 27264-8 $1.00

CIVIL WAR STORIES, Ambrose Bierce. 128pp. 28038-1 $1.00

ALICE'S ADVENTURES IN WONDERLAND, Lewis Carroll. 96pp. 27543-4 $1.00

O PIONEERS!, Willa Cather. 128pp. 27785-2 $1.00

FIVE GREAT SHORT STORIES, Anton Chekhov. 96pp. 26463-7 $1.00

FAVORITE FATHER BROWN STORIES, G. K. Chesterton. 96pp. 27545-0 $1.00

THE AWAKENING, Kate Chopin. 128pp. 27786-0 $1.00

HEART OF DARKNESS, Joseph Conrad. 80pp. 26464-5 $1.00

THE SECRET SHARER AND OTHER STORIES, Joseph Conrad. 128pp. 27546-9 $1.00

THE OPEN BOAT AND OTHER STORIES, Stephen Crane. 128pp. 27547-7 $1.00

THE RED BADGE OF COURAGE, Stephen Crane. 112pp. 26465-3 $1.00

A CHRISTMAS CAROL, Charles Dickens. 80pp. 26865-9 $1.00

THE CRICKET ON THE HEARTH AND OTHER CHRISTMAS STORIES, Charles Dickens. 128pp. 28039-X $1.00

NOTES FROM THE UNDERGROUND, Fyodor Dostoyevsky. 96pp. 27053-X $1.00

SIX GREAT SHERLOCK HOLMES STORIES, Sir Arthur Conan Doyle. 112pp. 27055-6 $1.00

WHERE ANGELS FEAR TO TREAD, E. M. Forster. 128pp. (Available in U.S. only) 27791-7 $1.00

THE OVERCOAT AND OTHER SHORT STORIES, Nikolai Gogol. 112pp. 27057-2 $1.00

GREAT GHOST STORIES, John Grafton (ed.). 112pp. 27270-2 $1.00

THE LUCK OF ROARING CAMP AND OTHER SHORT STORIES, Bret Harte. 96pp. 27271-0 $1.00

THE SCARLET LETTER, Nathaniel Hawthorne. 192pp. 28048-9 $2.00

YOUNG GOODMAN BROWN AND OTHER SHORT STORIES, Nathaniel Hawthorne. 128pp. 27060-2 $1.00

THE GIFT OF THE MAGI AND OTHER SHORT STORIES, O. Henry. 96pp. 27061-0 $1.00

THE NUTCRACKER AND THE GOLDEN POT, E. T. A. Hoffmann. 128pp. 27806-9 $1.00

THE BEAST IN THE JUNGLE AND OTHER STORIES, Henry James. 128pp. 27552-3 $1.00

THE TURN OF THE SCREW, Henry James. 96pp. 26684-2 $1.00

DUBLINERS, James Joyce. 160pp. 26870-5 $1.00

A PORTRAIT OF THE ARTIST AS A YOUNG MAN, James Joyce. 192pp. 28050-0 $2.00

DOVER · THRIFT · EDITIONS

All books complete and unabridged. All 5³⁄₁₆″ × 8¼″, paperbound. Just $1.00–$2.00 in U.S.A.

FICTION

THE MAN WHO WOULD BE KING AND OTHER STORIES, Rudyard Kipling. 128pp. 28051-9 $1.00

SELECTED SHORT STORIES, D. H. Lawrence. 128pp. 27794-1 $1.00

GREEN TEA AND OTHER GHOST STORIES, J. Sheridan LeFanu. 96pp. 27795-X $1.00

THE CALL OF THE WILD, Jack London. 64pp. 26472-6 $1.00

FIVE GREAT SHORT STORIES, Jack London. 96pp. 27063-7 $1.00

WHITE FANG, Jack London. 160pp. 26968-X $1.00

THE NECKLACE AND OTHER SHORT STORIES, Guy de Maupassant. 128pp. 27064-5 $1.00

BARTLEBY AND BENITO CERENO, Herman Melville. 112pp. 26473-4 $1.00

THE GOLD-BUG AND OTHER TALES, Edgar Allan Poe. 128pp. 26875-6 $1.00

THE QUEEN OF SPADES AND OTHER STORIES, Alexander Pushkin. 128pp. 28054-3 $1.00

THREE LIVES, Gertrude Stein. 176pp. 28059-4 $2.00

THE STRANGE CASE OF DR. JEKYLL AND MR. HYDE, Robert Louis Stevenson. 64pp. 26688-5 $1.00

TREASURE ISLAND, Robert Louis Stevenson. 160pp. 27559-0 $1.00

THE KREUTZER SONATA AND OTHER SHORT STORIES, Leo Tolstoy. 144pp. 27805-0 $1.00

ADVENTURES OF HUCKLEBERRY FINN, Mark Twain. 224pp. 28061-6 $2.00

THE MYSTERIOUS STRANGER AND OTHER STORIES, Mark Twain. 128pp. 27069-6 $1.00

CANDIDE, Voltaire (François-Marie Arouet). 112pp. 26689-3 $1.00

THE INVISIBLE MAN, H. G. Wells. 112pp. (Available in U.S. only.) 27071-8 $1.00

ETHAN FROME, Edith Wharton. 96pp. 26690-7 $1.00

THE PICTURE OF DORIAN GRAY, Oscar Wilde. 192pp. 27807-7 $1.00

NONFICTION

THE DEVIL'S DICTIONARY, Ambrose Bierce. 144pp. 27542-6 $1.00

THE SOULS OF BLACK FOLK, W. E. B. Du Bois. 176pp. 28041-1 $2.00

SELF-RELIANCE AND OTHER ESSAYS, Ralph Waldo Emerson. 128pp. 27790-9 $1.00

GREAT SPEECHES, Abraham Lincoln. 112pp. 26872-1 $1.00

THE PRINCE, Niccolò Machiavelli. 80pp. 27274-5 $1.00

SYMPOSIUM AND PHAEDRUS, Plato. 96pp. 27798-4 $1.00

THE TRIAL AND DEATH OF SOCRATES: FOUR DIALOGUES, Plato. 128pp. 27066-1 $1.00

CIVIL DISOBEDIENCE AND OTHER ESSAYS, Henry David Thoreau. 96pp. 27563-9 $1.00

THE THEORY OF THE LEISURE CLASS, Thorstein Veblen. 256pp. 28062-4 $2.00

PLAYS

THE CHERRY ORCHARD, Anton Chekhov. 64pp. 26682-6 $1.00

THE THREE SISTERS, Anton Chekhov. 64pp. 27544-2 $1.00

THE WAY OF THE WORLD, William Congreve. 80pp. 27787-9 $1.00

MEDEA, Euripides. 64pp. 27548-5 $1.00

THE MIKADO, William Schwenck Gilbert. 64pp. 27268-0 $1.00